Ex Libris

To Colin
love. Rosemary x.

A Country Brewery: Hook Norton 1849–1999

A COUNTRY BREWERY HOOK NORTON 1849–1999

∼

The story of a family brewing tradition, published to mark its 150th anniversary

DAVID EDDERSHAW

David Eddershaw

The Hook Norton Brewery Company Limited

First published in 1999 by The Hook Norton Brewery Company Limited,
Hook Norton, Banbury, Oxon, OX15 5NY

© The Hook Norton Brewery Company Limited, 1999

All rights reserved. No part of this publication may be reproduced, stored in a retrieval system, or transmitted in any form, or by any means, electronic, mechanical or photocopying, recording, or otherwise, without the prior permission of the publisher.

ISBN 0-953710-40-8

Printed by Oxuniprint, Oxford University Press

About the Author

David Eddershaw has lived in Chipping Norton, Oxfordshire, for more than thirty years. An historian and teacher by profession, he was for many years Education Officer and Assistant Director of the Oxfordshire County Museum Service. Now retired, he indulges his passion for telling people about the social history of Oxfordshire through lecturing and writing.

His other publications include *The Civil War in Oxfordshire*, Sutton 1995; *The Story of the Oxfordshire Yeomanry, 1798–1998*, Oxfordshire Yeomanry Trust, 1998; *Using Local History Sources – A Teacher's Guide* (with James Griffin), Hodder 1996.

CONTENTS

Acknowledgements   vi
Sources   vii
Family Tree   ix

1. JOHN HARRIS: farmer, maltster and brewer   1
2. MALTING   15
3. ALBAN CLARKE: expansion at the turn of the century   19
4. STEAM POWER IN THE BREWERY   53
5. PERCY FLICK: survival between the wars   61
6. DELIVERING THE BEER   81
7. BILL CLARKE: the revival of real ale   95
8. THE BREWING PROCESS   107
9. DAVID AND JAMES CLARKE: the brewery today and tomorrow   113
10. THE TIED ESTATE: Hook Norton pubs in 1999   123

ACKNOWLEDGEMENTS

David, Paula and James Clarke for allowing access to the archives of the Hook Norton brewery and to various family records, for providing additional information from their own knowledge, and for reading the text and correcting a number of innaccuracies. Any that remain are mine.

Barbara and Howard Hicks who helped with details about the brewery and the village, and who arranged for me to meet Doris Cadd, Nancy Pargeter, Minnie Padbury, Jan Sharpe, Phillis Tobin and Michael Turnock to whom I am also grateful for telling me so much from their long memories.

John Stratford, Fred Paintin and Fred Gardner for their memories.

Pauline Flick for a photograph and information about her father Percy Flick, and Peter Flick for information about the Flick family generally.

Richard Stevens for telling me about his uncle Harold Wyton and for supplying several photographs.

Christopher Tucker for an interesting correspondence about his grandfather Hargrave Walters.

Colin Bowden for information about the Hook Norton steam engine and Dave Roberts for patiently explaining the technical details and correcting my description of it. Any remaining errors are mine.

Martin Allitt of the Banbury Reference Library for helping to locate information about Percy Flick.

Staff of the Chipping Norton Branch Library.

Paul Cleal for typesetting and preparing this book for publication.

Dave Morris for several photographs at short notice.

Emma, Norma, and others who supplied me with coffee and made me feel welcome in the very friendly atmosphere of the brewery.

Cover picture: Detail of watercolour painting of the brewery by Joan Lawrence of Hook Norton. This Painting was presented to Bill Clarke to mark his 50th year with the firm.

SOURCES

MAIN SOURCES

The archives held at the brewery, including minute books, account ledgers, brewing books, letter books and wages books, as listed by the Business Archives Council in 1987, plus other items not listed.

Notes on the Clarke family and some correspondence and photographs in the possession of David and Paula Clarke.

Articles of Association and other records of the Hook Norton Brewery Company Ltd at Companies House.

Census Returns for Oxfordshire and Gloucestershire.

Commercial Directories for Banbury and Oxfordshire.

SECONDARY SOURCES

Bond, J. and Rhodes, J., *The Oxfordshire Brewer*, (Oxfordshire Museum Service, 1985)

Gourvish, T. R. and Wilson R. G., *The British Brewing Industry 1830–1980* (Cambridge, 1994)

Harrison, B., *Drink and the Victorians*, (Faber 1971)

Wood, V., *Licencees of Inns, Taverns and Beerhouses of Banbury* (Oxon Family History Society, 1998)

Woolley, R., *Midland Tales, No. 2 Hooky* (privately published 1978).

Promotional literature produced by the Hook Norton Brewery Company at various dates.

Bergström, T. and Hardman, M., *Beer Naturally*, (Bergström and Boyle for CAMRA, 1976)

Family Tree

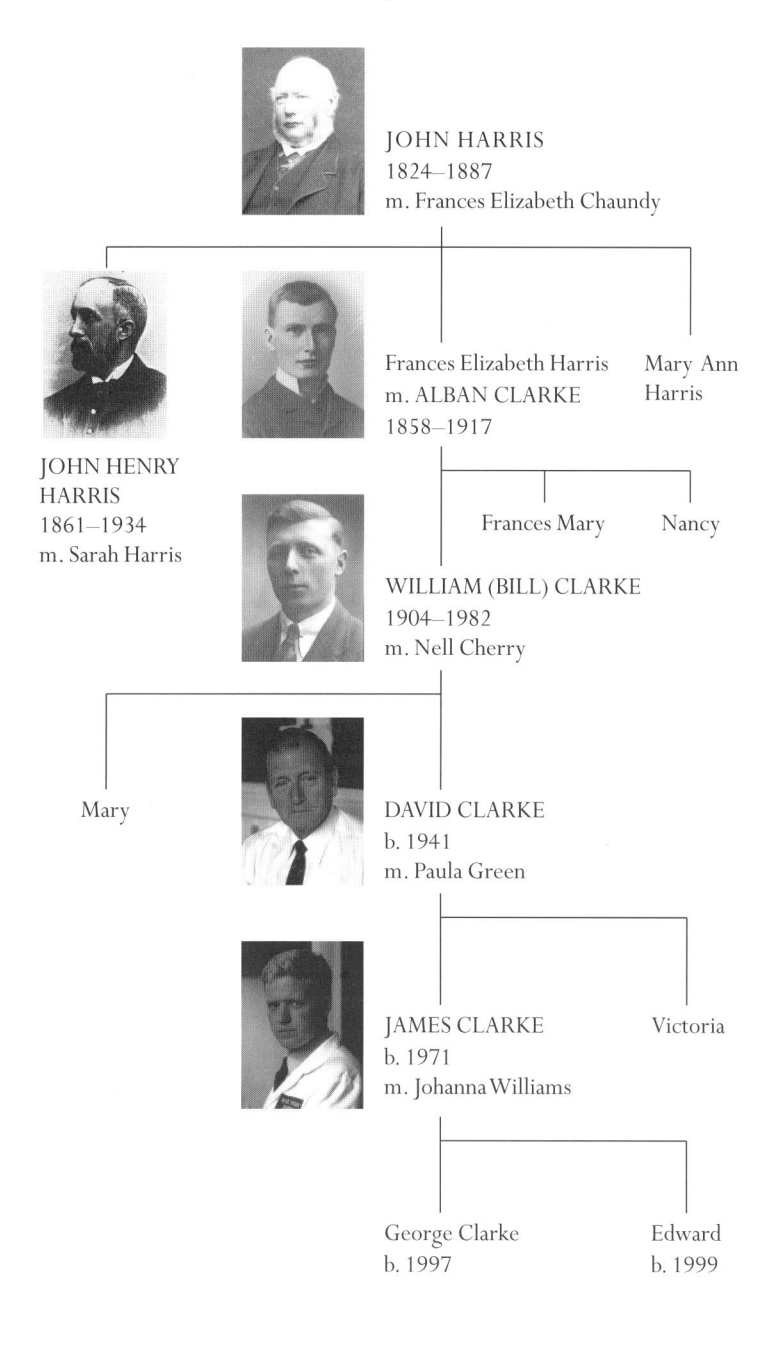

JOHN HARRIS
1824–1887
m. Frances Elizabeth Chaundy

JOHN HENRY HARRIS
1861–1934
m. Sarah Harris

Frances Elizabeth Harris
m. ALBAN CLARKE
1858–1917

Mary Ann Harris

Frances Mary

Nancy

WILLIAM (BILL) CLARKE
1904–1982
m. Nell Cherry

Mary

DAVID CLARKE
b. 1941
m. Paula Green

JAMES CLARKE
b. 1971
m. Johanna Williams

Victoria

George Clarke
b. 1997

Edward
b. 1999

1
JOHN HARRIS

Farmer, maltster and brewer

THE little hamlet of Chilson nestles into the hillside between Ascott under Wychwood and Charlbury with the dark line of Wychwood Forest dominating the horizon above it and the Evenlode winding happily through the sunlit valley below, accompanied today by the occasional train on the "Cotswold Line" between London and Worcester. No such disturbance broke the peace of the valley in 1824 when John Harris was born there.

His father, Henry Harris had married Elizabeth Bowl and now farmed one of Chilson's two farms, probably growing wheat, oats and barley and keeping some livestock, including the horses which pulled his wagons and ploughs. Barley was an important crop in the district and would be sold for malting. Hitchman's Brewery a few miles away in Chipping Norton was the largest commercial brewery in the area and had its own maltings where the grains of barley were sprouted and roasted to enable the brewer to convert the starch into sugars for use in brewing beer.

There were a number of reasons why brewing was on the increase in mid-nineteenth century Britain. One was that it was considered a

John Harris, 1824–1887

truly British beverage made from home grown raw materials. There was a strong lobby from farmers keen to encourage greater consumption, and therefore greater demand for their barley, and they were able to appeal to the patriotic myth that true Englishmen drank beer and ate beef, as opposed to the French who ate lamb and drank wine. There was a close affinity between farming, malting and brewing. Beer was also widely believed to be a wholesome drink, greatly to be preferred to gin for which there had been a craze among the poorer classes in the previous century, and beer drinking was seen as an antidote to this and positively beneficial to the nation's health – so much so that the Radcliffe Infirmary in Oxford had its own brewery at one time in order to provide beer for both patients and staff.

These considerations together with political arguments about Free Trade, persuaded the Duke of Wellington's government in 1830 to pass the Beer Act, sweeping away the power of local magistrates to grant or refuse beerhouse licences. Anyone who could afford the £2 2s. for a licence could now open a beerhouse and by 1838 no less than 46,000 new ones had sprung up all over the country. This huge increase in retail outlets naturally caused a growth of brewing, many of the beerhouse keepers brewing their own beer on the premises, and this in turn created new opportunities for the trade of malting. The rich farmlands of Oxfordshire were already noted as one of England's main barley growing areas, much of it being shipped down the Thames to supply the breweries of London while large amounts were also processed locally.

The only maltster in the village

It was against this background that John Harris went into malting. In 1849, shortly after his father died, he left the farm at Chilson to earn a living elsewhere. He moved the few miles to the larger village of Hook Norton where he purchased a moderate sized farm of 52 acres in the part of the village known as Scotland End. The attraction of this farm was that it included a malthouse where the previous owner had started to supply some of the village brewers – publicans, farmers and others who brewed at home – with malt. He did not make this move alone, for his mother and sister Mary came to share the new house and to look after him, as he was as yet unmarried. It may well have been his mother's money which helped to make the purchase and set him up in business, for she is described as a "fundholder" a few years later, possibly implying money inherited from her late husband.

Scotland End was a picturesque part of Hook Norton with small woods on the hillside around the few houses and a brook running in the valley below the farm, fed by springs rising in the fields only a short distance away. A photograph of the farmhouse itself taken some years later shows a stone building, probably sixteenth or seventeenth century in date with a thatched roof and walls of the local brown ironstone which is such an attractive feature of the village today. A single ground-floor window from this building still survives in the front wall of the present brewery, with stone dripmoulds typical of the period when the farmhouse was built.

Hook Norton at the time John Harris went to live there was a large village of about 1,500 people. It apparently still had annual horse and cattle fairs in mid-century and boasted five pubs and one of the newly licensed beerhouses. It had all the usual shopkeepers and tradesmen, making it self-sufficient for most of its daily needs – butcher, baker, two grocers one of whom was also a tailor (a strange combination), a draper, milliner, bonnet maker, two or three blacksmiths, several carpenters and a wheelwright, a bricklayer, a mason and a plumber and glazier, with many more. The Parish Clerk, Thomas Phipps, was also the local barber, while the unpaid Constable earned his living as a baker. There was both a church school and "British" school for dissenters, but children left school to go and earn their keep at an early age – there were many working as ploughboys on the local farms aged twelve or thirteen and one as young as eight. Farming was by far the largest occupation, no fewer than 45 people, including John Harris, describing themselves as farmers in the census of 1851. Their farms varied in size from a tiny 11 acre smallholding to the very large 645 acres of Nill Farm which employed 21 men and 10 boys. In Scotland End one of John Harris's neighbours was Mr Godson at Scotland Mount who farmed 440 acres, but most were under 100 and John Harris's 52 was fairly typical.

John Harris was the only maltster in the village. On the upper floor of the long low building close to the farmhouse, sacks of threshed barley from his own and other farms were converted into malt to be sold to local brewers. No-one in Hook Norton was described as a brewer in 1851, but that only signified that it was not a full-time occupation; there would have been plenty of people brewing beer on a small scale. The nearest to full-time brewers were the village innkeepers at The Sun, The Red Lion, The Bell, The Fleur de Lis (later renamed The Wheatsheaf), and The Gate Inn some distance away on the old drove road to Banbury, together with John Gibbard

John Harris in front of his malthouse, c.1880

who sold beer in the front room of his cottage in Down End licensed as a beerhouse. At this date it is likely that they were all brewing their own beer, mostly dark heavy stouts and porter, for which they would regularly buy malt and hops – and Harris soon became a dealer in hops as well as malt. The farms too would be brewing beer, especially the larger ones employing several labourers. It was customary for farmers to supply the men with beer or cider as they toiled in the fields at haytime and harvest and in larger amounts at the harvest home supper when all was safely gathered in. Special strong "Harvest Ales" would be brewed for these important and happy celebrations. Even in some of the private houses beer was being brewed for daily domestic use, the water supply from local springs and wells being of uncertain purity and many people finding it safer to drink a weak beer which had been boiled during the brewing process. In a large village like Hook Norton there would have been plenty of demand for John Harris's malt.

The beginning of brewing

In modern business jargon malt is a value-added product, the process of malting having increased the value of the original barley. A further step to maximise its potential value and the profit to be made from it was to use it to make beer himself rather than selling it to other brewers. It is very likely that Harris had brewed beer for his own use as soon as he arrived in Hook Norton but the important step from this to commercial brewing for sale came towards the end of 1856. He appears to have installed three round fermenting vessels and must also have had other brewing equipment to make this scale of production possible. It is unlikely that all this was fitted into the farmhouse and he was probably using another building attached to it or perhaps to the malthouse. The all-important water supply on which all good brewing depends was available on the site and is the same as used in the brewery today, drawn from wells underneath the present buildings.

One of the very few sources of evidence for John Harris's business

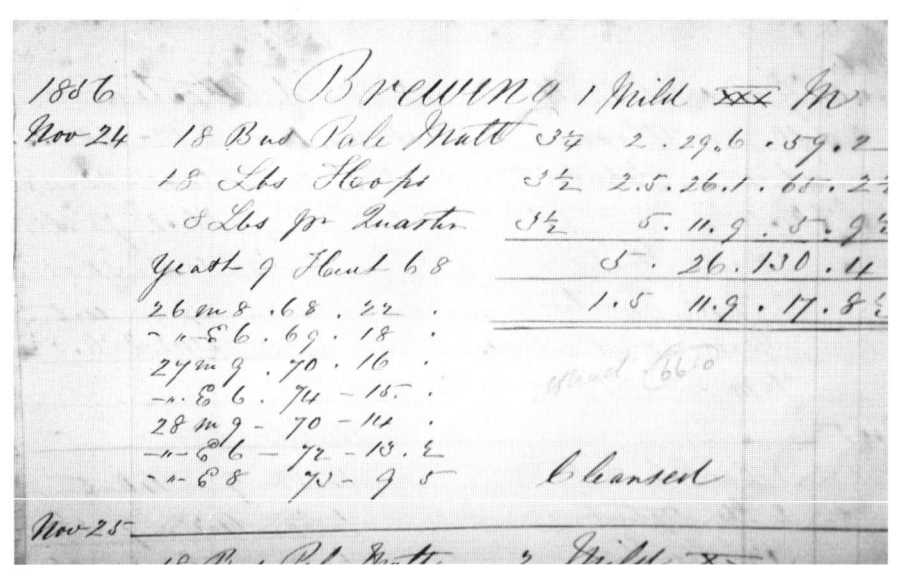

The first entry in John Harris's brewing book. It shows the recipe for Brewing number 1, dated November 24th 1856

are the brewing books he kept. In these he recorded the details of every brew: the type of beer being produced and the quantities and types of malt, hops and yeast used together with notes about timings, gravities and temperatures. Every brewing is numbered and dated, each new year commencing at number one. The first book begins late in 1856 with brew number 1 on November 24th that year, in which he used 18 bushels of his own pale malt, 18lbs of hops and 9lbs of yeast.

This first brew is described as "Mild XXX". Nearly all the beers are referred to as mild at this time, the range including beer, ale, porter, stout and something called "T beer". Bitter, with its higher hopping rate and light colour, was less well known in country districts at this date. In 1857, the first full year of brewing, porter and T beer were the most frequently brewed. For each brew the quantity and types of malt and hops are listed – "4 bushels Pale, 1 quarter 6 bushels Brown, 1¼ bushels Patent" are the malts used for a stout brewed in March 1857. As well as growing barley himself he seems to have been buying in from other farmers, supplies from Bloxham and Deddington and "Merry of Banbury" are mentioned. He usually records the use of each year's new malt in the autumn, often mixing it with last year's. Hops are usually "Loftus and Farnhams", "Kents" or "Sussex" often with the year of harvesting. He saved his own yeast culture but occasionally introduced others, mentioning on one occasion that yeast from The Bell Inn "worked well".

In May 1857 he started adding sugar to his brews, which was done by some brewers to improve fermentation. The addition of sugar was a controversial issue, disapproved of by some traditionalists and not generally accepted until after 1880, but Harris was regularly using 28lbs of sugar in every brew (and occasionally more) from 1857 onwards. It is sometimes referred to as "dark" sugar, which might imply caramel for colouring.

It was probably in 1860 that John Harris married Francis Elizabeth Chaundy, now like him in her thirties, but a girl he must have known since their childhood. She was the daughter of a farmer in Ascott under Wychwood, the next village to his own family at Chilson. Early in 1861 their son was born and christened John Henry after his father and grandfather.

At this stage, as well as brewing beer, John Harris was running his farm and malting barley and it is clear that he could not do all this single-handed. As early as 1851 he employed two men, and soon after he started brewing an assistant was making the entries in the brewing book and carrying out much of the work under Harris's instructions. The handwriting changes in June 1857 and some of the entries specially mention when the brew was done "by Mr Harris". In the first few years brewing usually took place on three consecutive days, which implies the use of three fermenting "rounds" in which the wort was left to ferment for several days before a new brew could be made. The frequency of brewing, however, is quite irregular, and probably reflects the fluctuating demand for John Harris's beer when he first set up the business. In the first winter of 1856-57 there is sometimes a gap of as much as a month between one brewing and the next, but in April 1857 demand began to pick up and there were brewings on no less than seventeen days in the month. In May and June it dropped back to three or four, and then got busy again in July and August. There were 96 brewings that year and the same number in 1858.

The second half of the nineteenth century was a boom period for brewing, national consumption of beer increasing steadily in spite of the efforts of the Temperance Movement, while raw material costs and taxation remained low. Public tastes were changing, however, moving away from the heavy dark porters and stouts to lighter beers, especially the increasingly popular pale ale produced by the brewers of Burton on Trent, where the quality of the local water supply was particularly suited to this kind of beer. It was not so easy to produce pale ale in other areas and John Harris experimented with it at the beginning of 1859 and again for just two brewings in January the following year. Perhaps he wasn't very successful, or local tastes had not yet caught up with such innovations, because very little was brewed until 1867 when it gradually became more frequent. The first bitter ale was brewed in 1864 as opposed to the milds brewed exclusively before that date. It was customary to store the beer for quite long periods in the brewery before it was sold to customers. The first brew of January 1873 was noted as "all gone by June 13th". After number 21 brewing on February 27th is a note saying "Sent out July 3rd to Woodstock, nice and mild". Beer was sometimes stored in large casks called pipes, twice the size of a hogshead, and there are references to several of these in the lower store and lower cellar in the 1870s. One such note says "hopped 2lbs each pipe" suggesting cask conditioning at this stage.

Brewing at this time was not an exact science and relied very much on trial and error, experience, and the brewer's ingenuity in trying to achieve the best conditions. Maintaining the correct temperature during fermentation was a particular problem. In the cold winter of 1870 John Harris tried to keep the temperature up by placing an iron brazier of hot coke next to the fermenting round. It must have helped because there are several further references to "Hot Coke" during February. Other methods of controlling the temperature included opening and closing the boards covering the top of the round. These were separate boards which could be removed singly or together to make fine adjustments. "Shut up close and cover up", "One board off", "3 boards on only" are typical references to this method. In 1874 "Attemperating" hose was used for the first time, which was simply a rubber hose pipe through which cold water was circulated around the fermenting vessel.

During the next ten years the brewery steadily increased its output and the buildings were enlarged to accommodate additional plant and equipment. By 1862 a fourth fermenting round was in use and another was added the next year. These five made it possible to brew greater quantities of beer at a time although the three day routine was retained, presumably leaving time to concentrate on farming activities, and malting after the barley harvest. A new apprentice was taken on in the late 1860s to be trained up as a brewer. This was John's nephew Walter Bowl, son of his older sister Ann who had married and moved away to Coln St Aldwyns in Gloucestershire. Walter now came to live in the farmhouse in Hook Norton and learn the art of brewing from his uncle. He was clearly successful at it, becoming head brewer for a time and working there for the rest of his life. Some years later Harris took on another of his nephews, Alban Alfred Clarke, one of his sister's children from her second marriage. Alban eventually married John's eldest daughter and was to play a leading part in the future of the brewery.

John Harris was clearly being successful in expanding his sales both locally and farther afield and by 1870 ten rounds were in production and there were 120 brewings that year, using several rounds each time so that total output was greatly increased. It is not certain where these new rounds were accommodated before 1872, which is said to be the date of the building of a new 3-storey brewery on the site. It may be that the enlarged brewery was built a few years earlier than this. A plan of a new building with a steam engine and brewing equipment dated 1880 suggests a further major enlargement in that year. A new malthouse had already been built in 1866 to increase the supply because of the greater quantity of beer being brewed.

Building a network of customers

Not all of the malt produced went into his own brewery, he was after all still advertising himself as a dealer in malt and hops as well as a brewer. Some malt was still being sold to small scale brewers in the locality – brewing publicans, farmers and the like. Small farmers were exempt from excise duty on the beer they brewed for their labourers while at work and so some of them kept up the custom of brewing in the farmhouse at least at harvest time. The number of publicans who brewed their own beer was beginning to decline nationally as they found it difficult to compete with the quality of beer now being produced consistently by commercial brewers, and this must have been the case in Hook Norton itself. But there were still some brewing publicans left and two of his customers in the 1880s were Mr Parker and Mr Meads, licensees of The Railway Inn and The Crown Inn, both in Droitwich, who each ordered three separate consignments of 14 sacks of malt in 1884, which had to be sent by rail from Chipping Norton station.

It was undoubtedly John Harris's skill in finding customers for his beer, not just locally but over a very wide area, that ensured the success of his brewery from the start. He supplied local publicans who did not brew for themselves, and in 1859 bought the beerhouse in Down End, Hook Norton, together with four cottages. Ten years later, in April 1869, he purchased the Pear Tree Inn just below the brewery in Scotland End for £260. These gave him at least the

Scotland End Farmhouse about 1890. John Harris bought the farm and its malthouse in 1849. The photograph shows Alban Clarke and others standing outside the farmhouse, which has become the office of John Harris & Co. This 17th century house was demolished to make way for the new brewery in 1899

beginning of a "tied estate" of guaranteed outlets, but the real backbone of his business at this time was probably the trade he built up with publicans of "free houses" and individual private customers outside the village. He employed agents called "outrides" who sought out customers in their areas, passed orders back to the brewery and collected payment. They were particularly important in establishing goodwill for the firm in these distant areas, calling on customers regularly in their pony traps provided by the brewery. Probably the first of the outriders was Richard Howse who was taken on by Harris in 1863 and was still working for his successors 30 years later. As the agency system developed, stores were estab-

The oldest part of the present brewery. This is probably the building put up by John Harris in about 1872. On the ground floor it incorporates a 17th century window from part of the the original farmhouse

lished in places like Shipston on Stour, Stratford on Avon and Banbury from which beer could be delivered by the outride to customers.

It is likely that John Harris made use of family connections in distant places to spread the network of sales. This may explain the Gloucestershire trade which lasted for many years, centered around Quenington and extending to Cheltenham. His sister had settled in Coln St Aldwyns and her second marriage made further links with this area as her new husband William Clarke had previously farmed in Quenington. The Clarke connection probably also accounts for the three kilderkins of ale sent to A. D. Clarke Esq in Chichester. In addition John Harris's wife's family, the Chaundys of Ascott under Wychwood, became good customers and his brother-in-law was named as an executor in his will. How the two publicans in Droitwich got to hear of him is harder to explain, and most surprising of all are private customers who were supplied with beer by rail in the 1880s as far away as London, Barnstaple and Doncaster.

Handing over to the next generation

By the time of John Harris's death in 1887 he had established a successful business under the name of John Harris & Company with a reputation for good beer, a wide network of agencies and customers, and a son and son-in-law already involved in the trade. He did not, however, leave the business directly to his 27 year-old son John Henry although in his will he expressed his "earnest desire that he shall become possessed of such part of my estate as is employed in carrying on my business, and may succeed and carry on the same". Instead he set up a trust to continue the business during the lifetime of his widow, the members being Frances Elizabeth herself, John Henry, John Chaundy of Ascott under Wychwood (Frances's brother) and Henry Harris (his nephew) who was a miller at Barton. He further stipulated that John Henry was to be "employed in assisting in the conduct of the business" at a salary to be agreed with the trustees, and that his nephews Walter Bowl and Alban Clarke "shall continue to give the same assistance as Managers which they have for a long time given to me". Perhaps these arrangements suggest that John Henry was reluctant to take over responsibility for the running of the business in spite of his father's "earnest desire" and that while he was involved to some extent and received a salary, the actual day to day management was in the hands of Alban Clarke and Walter Bowl. Such a situation was not unknown and many a successful father found he could not assume that his son would share the same enthusiasm for a business he had established. Whatever the circumstances behind the arrangement, it is clear that Alban Clarke was the one who eventually took the lead in running the brewery.

2

MALTING

A T the time John Harris moved to Hook Norton and set up as a maltster, malting was becoming a major industry in Britain supporting the expansion of brewing in the second half of the nineteenth century. Malt is one of the four main ingredients of beer. It was also subject to duty until 1880, making it an expensive item, so that its quality was of the utmost importance to brewers. This depends on the type of barley and the conditions of its growth, and on the skill of the maltster who processes it into malt.

At Hook Norton barley was originally grown on John Harris's farm and processed in his malthouse together with other barley purchased from local farmers. This gave control over the quality, as far as his skills allowed, and kept the cost as low as possible. Gradually, however, as production of beer expanded and more and more malt was needed, increasing amounts were bought in to supplement the brewery's own malting. From about the time of the First World War the farm was let to a tenant, and malting at Hook Norton was discontinued some years later.

Barley

Other grains have sometimes been tried, but barley remains the best for beer. In the nineteenth century most of the barley grown in England went into brewing and the rest was used for cattle feed or for distilling. Grain with a high starch content was required for brewing, and a traditional favourite is the variety called Maris Otter, which is used at Hook Norton today because of its flavour, although its yield of sugar is not quite as high as some more modern varieties. Barley grows best on light soils without too high a nitrogen content and East Anglia became the main producing area, although a good deal was also grown in the south midlands, Oxfordshire producing a considerable quantity for local use and for shipping down the Thames to London breweries. A directory of 1864 lists no less than 59 maltsters in the county including John Harris. Nearly half of this number were in the Banbury–Chipping Norton area where the soil was particularly suitable for this crop. From the 1880s increasing amounts of foreign barley were imported as free trade and the development of agriculture and transport enabled foreign producers to compete favourably in the home market.

The malting process

The main function of barley in brewing is to provide natural sugars which can react with yeast to form alcohol during fermentation. To achieve this the grains of barley have first to be converted into malt by inducing them to sprout and then arresting further growth at the point where the enzymes which will convert the starch to sugar are at their greatest. The process takes place in specially designed industrial buildings called malthouses. In John Harris's day the work was done by hand, mostly by men with wide wooden maltshovels for spreading and turning the grain and wearing special slippers which were more suitable than their normal working boots. In a modern malting the process has been mechanised and speeded up.

First the grains were thoroughly soaked in water in a large tank or "steep". Then they were spread several inches deep on the floor of a

Malting

Workmen from the malthouse. They are holding the characteristic wide wooden maltshovels with which they turned the grain on the malthouse floor

vast open hall where they stayed for about a week, being turned with the shovels from time to time as they begin to germinate. It is the natural process of germination which releases enzymes, but if allowed to proceed the sugar will be produced in the maltings instead of in the mash tun. When the crucial stage is reached, the grain is transferred to the tiled floor of the kiln room, and heat from the kiln stops further germination. The malt is then roasted to varying degrees which will affect the colour and type of beer for which it is eventually used.

3

ALBAN CLARKE

Expansion at the turn of the century

ALBAN Clarke's links to the Harris family seem complex today, dating as they do from a period when village families often became linked in several generations and marriages between cousins were common. The comparative isolation of village communities like those of Chilson, Shorthampton and Ascott under Wychwood, the lack of leisure time and the limitations of travel for most people reduced the opportunities for finding a partner outside the immediate locality.

One of John Harris's sisters, Ann Harris, had married Henry Bowl, (possibly one of her cousins, as her mother was a Bowl) and gone to live in Coln St Aldwyns, Gloucestershire, where Henry ran a grocer's shop. They had five children between 1846 and 1850. When Henry died Ann soon married again, this time to William Clarke, a prosperous farmer in the village who had also been married previously and had four children of his own. The union between the two families was further strengthened when Ann's eldest daughter and William's eldest son from their first marriages also married each other. William and Ann then went on to have three

Alban Clarke, 1858–1917

more children of whom Alban Alfred Clarke was the second, born in Coln St Aldwyns in 1858. It was a large household even for a farmhouse, and when the census enumerator visited them in 1861 there were no less than 15 people living in it. This included four servants, implying a comfortable, if crowded, lifestyle. There was still room for a visitor, and Ann's sister Mary Ann Harris was staying with her at the time.

Alban Clarke

Walter Bowl, Ann's youngest son from her first marriage, had gone to live with his uncle John Harris to learn the art of brewing, and he was joined a few years later by Alban Clarke, youngest son of her second marriage. After living in the brewery house in Hook Norton as part of the family for more than ten years, Alban eventually married John Harris's eldest daughter, and his own cousin, Frances Elizabeth Harris.

John Henry Harris

In his will John Harris set up a trust to run the business after his death rather than leaving it outright to his son John Henry. Both Walter Bowl and Alban Clarke were to continue as managers and John Henry Harris was to be involved in the business, but his precise role is not easy to discover. What does seem clear from the surviving records is that Alban Clarke in every practical sense took over the

John Henry Harris, 1861–1934

running of the business of John Harris & Co, as the firm was styled. John Henry and his two sisters were partners with Alban but he played the leading part. He filled the role of Managing Director and appears to have been energetically involved in every aspect of the work. On a day-to-day basis it was Alban who handled the management of the business; he planned and supervised the building of the new brewery and although both men are named as "managing directors" of the new limited company established in 1900, Alban received a higher salary. John Henry is a rather shadowy figure in the background at this period, emerging more prominently after Alban's death in 1917, and continuing his long association with the brewery until his own death in 1934. He is the longest serving male member of the family connected with the brewery, yet ironically the one about whom least is known. It may have been his wish to play a subsidiary role or he may have been pushed into it by his more energetic brother-in-law. The brief mentions of John Henry in the records before 1915 suggest that he may have been involved with the "stables" department and concerned with the deliveries and he was probably responsible for the family farm attached to the brewery. Walter Bowl continued to work in the brewery but does not seem to have been a partner or director of the new company.

Alban Clarke: brewery manager, country sportsman and parish councillor

Alban kept diaries for parts of the years 1897 to 1900. Like many people then and later, he started each year with regular daily entries, but after some months they usually get thinner and then cease altogether. The 1901 diary is completely blank. Such entries as there are in the others, however, give a lively picture of his busy and varied lifestyle, mixing together notes about the brewery and its staff, farming operations, fishing and shooting and involvement in various village activities. On a typical day in January 1897, in addition to supervising the brewing he interviewed a tenant who wanted his rent reduced, reprimanded one of the brewery employees about his conduct and noted the absence through illness of another. Then there was a meeting to attend in the village about a new road, and finally he went shooting and bagged a brace of partridges.

Two weeks before he had listed the names of four men "and young Gibbs" who had helped drive partridges on South Hill. They were probably brewery employees. Some of the birds were later given to friends as presents, apparently well "hung" as two brace killed on the 5th were given away on the 16th. On the 18th January he recorded (with a note of pride that would not be shared today) "Killed 12 larks with one shot in Red Lane", and on the following weekend, shooting at Deane with Mr Toy they bagged 1 mallard, 1 fieldfare, 30 rabbits, 1 pheasant and 13 partridges on Saturday, and "30 larks round the brewery" on Sunday. He was not totally insensitive to other ways of enjoying wild birds, however, as in May he records hearing nightingales singing. Occasionally the farm gets a mention: "March 3rd boy bitten by horse" (this might have been in the brewery stables). "March 6th cow calved. March 8th W. Fenemore bought 7 pigs."

Sandwiched between these events are items about the brewery: "April 23rd drilling oats in Ivy House; brewing this night. April 24th finished drilling oats in Bourne", which gives a good indication of how hard he worked. He spent Saturday March 27th "Planning a big week's work", and subsequent entries explain it:

29th, at mashing and amongst brewing all day.
30th, at mashing.
31st, at mashing; shot a rat.
April 1st, at mashing.
2nd, at malting up.

There was no time for other sport that week, apart from shooting the unfortunate rat which was probably one of the many infesting every malthouse and brewery in the land. (In much more recent times men remembered Monday mornings at the brewery when a couple of Jack Russell terriers were brought in to catch any rats unfortunate enough to have fallen into the empty copper or other vessels over the weekend.) There were a number of occasions when extra brewing took place at night: "April 5th, brewing till 12 midnight". Perhaps he was also up as late a few weeks after this when he records "Self and Brotheridge to Chipping Norton Licensed Victuallers Dinner". (It is noticeable that Alban rather than John Henry attended this.) Alban was personally involved with every aspect of the brewery and its problems, including one of the most unpleasant which was the effluent finding its way into the brook running through Scotland End. No doubt residents at this end of the village were as concerned as the official from the Thames Water Conservancy that something should be done about it and in February 1897 Alban called in Mr Beavington the local plumber to help him sort it out. After clearing out the cesspit and carting away manure he recorded in the diary: "February 19th, sample of effluent to Mr Wood. Brook clear but slimy", and the next day "Amongst the

Alban Clarke in typical pose with shotgun and a group of men out shooting near the brewery

drains. Arranged lavatory fittings with Beavington. Used manure cart and opened all trenches".

He was equally energetic in his involvement with the life of the village. As a member of Hook Norton's recently elected Parish Council in 1897, the year of Queen Victoria's Diamond Jubilee, he attended several meetings about the celebrations to be held in the village. Free beer was often provided for men attending the customary Jubilee dinner, so he would no doubt be seen as an important member of the organising committee. It was decided to erect a new flagpole on St Peter's church as a permanent memorial and the remark in his diary for June 10th "Flag episode" may refer to the actual erection of the flagpole on top of the church tower. The congregation of St Peter's had already installed some new church bells, and he had attended a meeting of the Bell Committee earlier in the year. He was at a Conservative meeting in March and a Village Club meeting at The Sun in May, when there was a discussion about affiliation to the Oddfellows Society. As summer approached, the village cricket team got ready for the new season and Alban not only attended meetings "at the Ground" but took part in two practices and played in a 12-a-side match. He had earlier paid £2 "for the cricket Ground", which suggests that the team rented or perhaps was trying to purchase its own field. He was active in support of several village sporting clubs, giving "G. Fox 10s. for a Quoits sub" and going to several sports meetings and a cyclists' meeting.

Involvement with sporting and other organisations in the village was a family tradition (continued to the present day). One of the things for which John Henry Harris is remembered is his support for the founding of the Hook Norton Volunteer Fire Brigade in 1896, following a rick fire on the brewery farm. A new horse-drawn engine was purchased and in 1897 the nineteen volunteer firemen had an outing with it to Chipping Norton. The *Oxfordshire Weekly News* on April 15th reported that "the Brigade are particularly indebted to Messrs J. Harris and Co of the Brewery for their kindness in contributing the presence of a pair of splendid bay horses for the journey. The Brigade are also very grateful to the gentlemen of the firm for their kind interest and for many favours received at their hands."

Building the new brewery

John Harris had already enlarged his brewery in the 1870s and '80s from a small domestic operation to a commercial business, and within a few years of his death the family undertook an ambitious new building programme which was to transform it again, more than doubling its size and capacity. In doing this they were following a national trend, many other breweries up and down the country having built themselves new, enlarged premises during the boom period in the second half of the nineteenth century. If anything they were a little late in doing so as the boom was slowing down and, especially in many rural areas, was being replaced by a period of depression at the end of the century to do with imports of foreign corn and meat. New technology applied to farming and transport like reaping machines, railways and refrigerated ships, meant that the products of the American prairies or the pastures of New Zealand could compete with home grown produce. Alban Clarke, however, was fortunate that in Hook Norton at this time new industrial technology was providing an alternative to farming so that instead of depression, the village was flourishing, with new employment opportunities for those displaced from the land – and new opportunities for marketing beer. In the late 1880s the Hook Norton Ironstone Partnership was formed to exploit the natural resources of the area, and quarries were opened up at the eastern end of the village. The Brymbo Steel Company moved in in 1897 and erected kilns for processing the ore on site. All this made possible the extension of the railway line, which had reached Chipping Norton in the 1850s, to Hook Norton and on to King's Sutton and Banbury. It was no simple undertaking and the work took many years. The Hook Norton section was particularly problematic because of the nature of the local geology which continued to cause periodic landslips even after the line was eventually completed. The approach to the village required a tunnel, a deep cutting and a magnificent viaduct with high stone pillars, all of which was finally opened in 1887, the year John Harris died.

The navvies who constructed this part of the line must themselves had boosted sales of J. Harris & Co's beer considerably, but the longer term benefit was in maintaining the prosperity of the village and in providing a vital means of transport for raw materials, equipment and casks of beer to and from the brewery. The Ironworks also provided employment and increased demand for beer. At the same time raw materials for brewing were becoming cheaper with the abolition of duty on malt in 1880 and the availability of imported supplies. Such an optimistic economic background no doubt gave the firm confidence to invest in a major expansion of the brewery.

Alban Clarke led this initiative and supervised every stage of the work. He began modestly with a new bottling room, store and washing shed in 1890, followed by a stable block four years later. They were designed and built by a well known local builder Alfred Groves of Milton under Wychwood, and the stables were to include eight enclosed stalls for drayhorses, two loose boxes and two smaller stalls plus a harness room. This was probably intended to separate the brewery from the farm, providing it with its own accommodation for the working horses rather than keeping them at the farm.

The next stage came in 1896 with the building of new offices. The work took a year from planning to completion and for this a new builder was employed, W. J. Bloxham, Builder, Contractor and Merchant, of the Steam Sawmills and Joinery Works at 1 Warwick Road, Banbury. He produced eight pages of coloured plans and elevations which included such details as the attractive "dogtooth" design in red and blue bricks running around the eaves, and the ornamental datestone above the office entrance. The internal fittings included lavatories for the staff, steam heating pipes and "cork carpet" in the offices. Alban's diary records "moving safes into new offices" on June 7th 1897.

Before this was done he was preparing for the final stage – the building of a completely new, larger brewery on the site of the existing one. It was to be six storeys high instead of three, typical of many Victorian "tower" breweries. The height was necessary so that once the liquor had been pumped up to the top of the "tower", gravity would feed it from one process to the next. The pumping, from wells below the brewery floor, was to be done by a new steam engine installed for the purpose. An undertaking of this scale was not something that could just be planned with a local builder, and the firm of William Bradford & Sons, Architects, of Regent Street London, was engaged to design the new brewery and manage the contracts for the building and plant. Bradford was one of the leading brewery architects of his day, particularly noted for his belief that brewery buildings should be imposing examples of architecture as well as being funtional. His earlier projects included Stansfield's Swan Brewery at Fulham and Harvey's Bridge Wharfe Brewery at Lewes, and his firm was actually involved in the building of the very large Star Brewery for Shipstones of Nottingham at the same time as his work at Hook Norton. Mr Bradford himself was at the brewery on May 17th 1898 to go over the specifications for the last time and Alban instructed him to commence getting tenders immediately. By July 29th work started on digging the foundations for the new copper house.

Problems and delays

The whole plan was complicated by the fact that Alban could not afford to stop brewing while the work was in progress; the firm's customers had to be supplied or he would lose them. Bradford's specification included careful plans to keep the old brewery in action, even to the extent of shoring it up while the adjoining building was demolished and rebuilt. Brewing would somehow go on amid the dust and commotion of the building site. Then, according to the plan, all the new plant would be fitted into the the new copper house and brew house so that brewing could be transferred there without a break, before the old brewery was pulled down to make way for a new fermenting house. Some of the new fermenting vessels would have to be fixed temporarily in the racking room while this was happening.

Bloxham's of Banbury were again employed to do the building work, using local stone with cast iron pillars and other structural elements coming from Samuelson's foundry in Banbury. The stone is said to have come from quarries at Swerford and Sibford and some

Alban Clarke

Workmen in front of the new copperhouse, 1899. The old brewery building on the right was shored up so that brewing could continue while the copperhouse was being built

of the men from the brewery helped bring it on carts to Hook Norton, their time being carefully logged by Alban Clarke and deducted from Mr Bloxham's final account. Some items were sent by rail, and he noted that three of his men spent eight hours at the station on October 6th loading the new Hop Back, while another man helped unload it at the brewery. When a "mortar mill" had to be brought from the station at Chipping Norton it took 2 men and a boy with 7 horses a whole day to haul it to the brewery, and he commented that it would have taken half that time if it had been sent to Hook Norton station instead.

Alban's diaries are full of comments about the progress, or lack of it, at every stage of the work, clearly showing his mounting anxiety and frustration at the delays which occurred. On May 8th 1899 he wrote "A. A. Clarke here at 6. Buxton and Thornley's men at 8, fitting new wort pump. Absent from 1 o'clock", and the next day "Engineers not here till 8 a.m., absent in afternoon." On another occasion he complained to the men about their late start (8.30) and sent a telegram to their firm to complain. The reply was that they were held up waiting for delivery of copper piping. He wrote in his diary "Why do we not have engineer's day vouchers?"

While this was going on Bloxham's men were working to complete the copper house and building a new chimney for the boiler. As it grew higher, elaborate wooden scaffolding was erected. On May 11th, (appropriately Ascension Day) Alban climbed to the top to witness the first of the large capping stones being laid. On the 19th he mentioned "Lighting fires in the boiler first time". After some more time spent "touching up shaft" and the long delay while the fitters were awaiting delivery of piping, there is a triumphant entry on June 26th "First brewing by steam!"

Work then started on demolishing the old brewery where brewing had continued up to this time. Three days were spent "pulling down front of old brewery and old chimney", but Alban was having problems with some of the new equipment. Buxton & Thornley, of Waterloo Works Burton on Trent, were the main contractors for supplying and installing all the brewery plant and machinery. They were a firm who specialised in such work and had developed and patented certain items themselves, including a pump and an ingenious form of gearing for steam engines, an example of which was fitted to the engine they installed at Hook Norton in October 1899. Their expertise did not prevent Alban Clarke having plenty to complain about, however. The wort copper coil (piping used to maintain the temperature) leaked and the diary records "Walters and man 2 or 3 hours mending same". The next day "Coil burst up again. Walters working from 6 to 9 at it", and on the third day there is a note of sarcasm in the remark "Walters Patent Coil affair – broke again, compelling brewing in Under Back". Walters was absent "alleged illness" when further trouble occurred a few weeks later, and on September 6th Alban "sent Walters an ultimatum" the outcome of which is unrecorded. Hargrave Walters had been hired by Buxton and Thornley to oversee the work. He was a young engineer who specialised in brewery plant installations, having recently completed a similar contract at Style and Winch's brewery in Maidstone, where he also met and married a local girl. He brought his young wife to Hook Norton and lodged in rented rooms near the church, and here their first child was born in June 1900. Such preoccupations might explain his apparent lack of concentration at the brewery. He was described in later life as "a very self-assured and blunt Yorkshireman" and it seems likely that there was a clash between two strong personalities when he and Alban met.

Other concerns

While such entries show what an anxious time he was having at the brewery keeping an eye on every stage of the work, breathing down the necks of the contractors as well as maintaining the output of beer, somehow Alban also found time to indulge his passion for shooting and fishing. Out early in the morning shooting rabbits, he was often fishing in the evenings. He had acquired a new bicycle in April 1897 and probably used it on his expeditions to Wigginton where he caught trout and gudgeon. In July "the ladies" went fishing – perhaps his wife Frances and her sister Mary Ann – and caught seven fish weighing 3lbs 2ozs, and in August he was out crayfishing in the local streams which is usually done at night.

The family farm was an integral part of the business at this time, and while John Henry probably ran it, Alban also lent a hand at busy times. Among the pages of the diary recording progress on the new brewery buildings are notes about time spent in harvesting and thrashing. At the end of April 1899 he spent three days assisting at the thrashing of a wheat rick, and a note on the 29th says "thrashing – 30 rats and 1,000 mice". In July there was haymaking and he records the names of men working late, probably brewery employees as well. It was good weather for haymaking that year, very hot for two weeks until it broke on the 22nd. In August two days were spent carting wheat, one for oats and another for barley. The barley would later be taken to his malthouse to be malted for use in the brewery and the oats and hay provided fodder for the brewery horses and for those used on the farm.

Somehow there was also time for cricket. He went to Oxford in May to see the Australians play the University in The Parks, and two days later records that the match ended in a draw. Perhaps inspired by watching the tourists and the young gentlemen of Oxford, he himself had a practice with the village team at the end of the week. He continued to follow the Australians during the summer, copying their scores from the newspapers into his diary. On May 26th, when he finds time to shoot rabbits as well as meet with the contractors at the brewery, he writes "Australians beat Lancashire by many runs".

On top of all this there was still the brewing to attend to and it is not surprising that there was sometimes difficulty in keeping up supplies. On August 18th, also the last week of harvesting on the farm, he writes "No stout in stock". Brewing went on late into the night during the following week and a note on the 24th says "finished brewing at 2 a.m.".

"Everything moves painfully slowly"

Alban was constantly urging the contractors to speed up their progress on the new buildings but even when this happened further delays occurred with the installation of the brewing equipment. As the year 1900 drew to a close, he wrote to William Bradford the architect "Will you please oblige by hurrying on the completion of the brewery plant. The man who was here to cover the pipes has run away and the work is at a standstill", and on the same day he sent off another letter to Buxton & Thornley: "We must beg you to push on with the completion of the hot liquor tank and the other things in arrears. It would be a great convenience to us to finish off promptly". It was not simply a question of completing the work, there were all sorts of teething problems when the new equipment was first used. The hot liquor tank leaked and "although the lagging has been stripped off and bolts tightened, to the injury of the teak, yet it started leaking all round again yesterday". Alban was convinced that millboard had been used instead of rubber in the joints. Then he had to complain that the new brick floor in the racking room had to be taken up and relaid because the builder did not use enough cement in the mortar: "Please note that we must not be charged with this work". A new lift had been supplied and installed by the firm of Waygood & Co but "it gets out of working order after a few loads have been lowered. We only load 14cwt, although once our man in ignorance lowered 22cwt. We would like Mr Bradford to see it". Fortunately, Mr Bradford's inspection showed that the fault was due to the lift not having been installed quite vertically, rather than the "ignorance" of the brewery employee who overloaded it. (This Waygood's lift, powered by line shafting from the steam engine, is still in use a hundred years later.) On another occasion there was an accident when hoisting the rollers for the grist mill up to the top floor of the new building "the tackle broke away and the roll fell from the top, crashing through the temporary roof and narrowly missing two men", but Alban's concern seems to be about damage to the roller and the possible delay rather than for the men: "We should be glad to know that the roll has sustained no damage before being fixed. We are pleased to know that you are coming down next week. Everything moves painfully slowly."

Even when everything was finally in place and working another dispute arose with Buxton & Thornley, who demanded payment for a steam heating coil costing £59 10s. which Alban maintained had never been ordered. The argument became quite personal when Mr G. Thornley in return refused to pay his personal account for £6 8s. 6d. for beer purchased from the brewery and delivered to his home address. Solicitors were engaged and the case was about to be heard at Banbury Magistrates Court when in a last minute exchange of telegrams both side agreed to drop their claims.

In spite of all these difficulties, the new brewery and its equipment was a triumph for all involved. The building remains largely unaltered a hundred years later and even some of the original plant is still in use, most notably the Buxton & Thornley 25 horse-power steam engine which continues to do its daily work.

The final accounts were eventually agreed and settled, the total cost being £19,360 1s. 11d. made up as follows:

W. J. Bloxham, building brewhouse, copper house, malt stores, cellars and tunnel, fermenting house, cask washing shed, loading out stage	£9,744	15s.	0d.
Buxton & Thornley, supplying and fitting brewing plant and equipment, including horizontal steam engine	£7,669	8s.	11d.
William Bradford & Sons, preparing drawings, specifications and contracts, supervising work and certifying the accounts.	£973	19s.	0d.
Waygood & Co, power lift	£47	10s.	0d.
R. Morton & Co, two refrigerators	£250	5s.	0d.
R. Ramsden & Son, fermenting squares	£219	4s.	0d.
Galloways Ltd, boiler	£330	0s.	0d.
J. Hawley Ltd, water heater	£125	0s.	0d.
	£19,360	1s.	11d.

Raising the money

Raising nearly £20,000 to pay for this work was a considerable undertaking for a small country brewery, but it was achieved in two ways: by borrowing on the security of the tied houses and other property owned by John Harris & Co and then by forming a new limited liability company and issuing shares.

Between 1898 and 1900 about £35,000 was raised through mortgages and unsecured loans, and this would have supplied the immediate cash to pay for the new brewery. William Toy played a significant part in this operation, being involved in arranging about half of the amount raised, including an unsecured personal loan of £1,000. Toy was a well established solicitor, partner in the Chipping Norton firm of Wilkins & Toy, and was elected mayor of the borough in 1903 and again in 1917. He was already acting for John Harris & Co, prosecuting bad debts etc, and as a solicitor who was also a much respected figure in the community his advice would undoubtedly have been sought on financial matters by many individuals and by the trustees of several family bequests. It was no doubt by this

A remarkable photograph taken in 1899 showing the men employed in building the new brewery posed on the scaffolding. Builders, carpenters, stonemasons, etc., carry the tools of their trades and there are others in rather more formal dress, perhaps foremen, as well as some smartly dressed boys who are presumably just there for the photograph. The gentleman in the foreground wearing a straw boater and carrying a roll of plans may be William Bradford the London architect. Notice the wooden scaffolding made of fir poles lashed together with ropes.

means that they were persuaded to invest their money in the brewery by lending on the security of its properties at rates of interest between 4 and 5 per cent. Among the list of such loans are several well known Chipping Norton names from that period: Benjamin Bowen (glove manufacturer and mayor in 1897), Keck, Pettipher, Burbidge (prosperous tradesmen), O'Kelly (the doctor), Wilkins (solicitor and Toy's partner), and, most interesting of all, A.W. S. Hitchman of Hitchman's Brewery in Chipping Norton who must have been one of Hook Norton's chief competitors and yet was prepared to lend money to assist the building of his rival's new premises. Other names on the list, not linked to William Toy, are those of family relatives like the Chaundys of Ascott under Wychwood and Henrietta Bowl of Fairford, one of Alban's step-sisters. His step-brother Walter Bowl who had worked with him in the brewery for many years also lent £1,000. Even long serving employees like Richard Howse and F. Stratford made personal loans.

The Hook Norton Brewery Company Ltd

The new company was registered on July 12th 1900 in the name of The Hook Norton Brewery Company Ltd, with a nominal share capital of £52,000. £25,000 was in ordinary shares held by the family – John Henry Harris, Francis Elizabeth (Alban's wife), Mary Ann Harris and Alban Clarke – as part payment for the sale of the old company of J. Harris & Co which had been valued at £76,000. There was also a cash payment, and the new company took over the debts of the old one (chiefly the recent mortgages). In order to start paying off these mortgages, £27,000 was raised by a private issue of 5½ per cent Preference shares which were offered for sale at £10 each. Alban had written to eighteen of the company's agents in June asking for the names of customers and potential customers in their areas who would be likely to buy shares in the company and there was no shortage of subscribers from this and other sources. In the last few days of July, just before the offer closed, he answered an inquiry from a Banbury solicitor by saying "it may not be too late to get your client £400 allotted in our preference shares if you apply in the usual way by Saturday, although more than the required amount has already been applied for".

The success of this private issue was helped by the confidence in brewing profits nationally which made people rush to take up shares in breweries whenever they were offered for sale, and the reputation which the firm of John Harris & Co had already built up locally, earning profits (according to the new company's prospectus) of over £4,000 a year in 1898 and 1899.

The new directors were Alban Clarke, John Henry Harris (both described as managing directors) and William Toy. Although two "managing directors" were named, it was clear from the outset that Alban was the senior of the two and the main responsibilities of management fell on him. His remuneration was set at £500 per annum, whereas John Henry received £350. William Toy was to receive £100 and was appointed Chairman, and his firm of Wilkins & Toy were the Company's solicitors. George Groves became the first Company Secretary, a post he would hold for many years.

The Company made reasonable profits in the years immediately following its formation, meeting its obligations to shareholders and customers, and beginning to pay off its debts inherited from the old company. A further issue of 1,500 new "B" Preference shares was authorised in 1903 to redeem the mortgages on its property, but only 750 were offered for sale, and an offer of 450 Debentures at £50 in 1910, although authorised, does not seem to have been taken up. However, sales figures which peaked in 1903 then began to decline, and after 1907 profits were so low that no dividend could be paid on the ordinary shares from then until the middle of the First World War.

This was a difficult period for brewing nationally. The Boer War brought a sudden increase in the Beer Tax in 1900 from 6s. 3d. to 7s. 9d. per standard barrel and there were signs that the nineteenth century boom was over. Beer sales in the pubs declined because of a growth in rival attractions such as football and other organised sports, cycling, cheap railway excursions and even seaside holidays. None of these precluded drinking but they made alternative demands on time and on the family budget in a period when wages were low. National consumption of beer fell every year from 1899 to 1909. Lloyd George's famous budget in that year raised beer taxes again to help pay for the introduction of Old Age Pensions (revenue from this source doubled after 1910). The cost of licences both for brewing and retailing beer increased.

Management strategies for success

Against this background survival of the new company would depend largely on the quality of management and the skills with which Alban Clarke could guide it through the difficulties, reducing costs,

The first letterhead of the Hook Norton Brewery Company Ltd, *c.* 1900. It shows an artist's impression of the new brewery.

building up reserves and maintaining sales. He took these responsibilities seriously, setting out in the back of his diary for 1900 a list of the measures to be taken to make the firm more efficient. Typically for a brewer, he described the areas where waste was identified as "leakages".

His strategy for improvement involved cutbacks in several areas, including labour costs. "Less men in brewery when new place is working. Re-arrange men's duties. Re-arrange stable management. Abolish all labour which is not required to work brewery business." What today would be recognised as "out-sourcing" was recommended for the farm, previously an integral part of the business: labour costs would be saved by letting as much as possible of the land instead of farming it directly. Corn and straw for the brewery horses should be bought from brewery customers and "purchased by weight only". Barley should not be over stocked, it should be bought "more hand to mouth than hitherto", and hops should be bought two or three times in the year and later in the season.

The agencies and stores which were the basis of both the private and tied trade outside the immediate Hook Norton area were to be looked at carefully "to see how they pay"; the depot in Stratford on Avon in particular might be closed, the pub let to a tenant and private customers supplied from the store at Shipston on Stour. The agents themselves were "to be in touch with every debtor and to advise the office immediately of change of residence or doubtful circumstances." Customers' accounts were to be examined regularly "and dealt with on merits" (i.e. the financial standing of the customer), and the company's own accounts with tradesmen were to be kept down to the lowest limits. He notes that a blacksmith "on ground" – presumably one on the permanent staff at the brewery – would be a great saving, which is at variance with his "out-sourcing" policy elsewhere. The recovery of empty casks, always a preoccupation in the brewing trade because of the capital tied up in them (they were valued at £1,185 in the 1899 balance sheet), was to be improved by stricter supervision of the draymen who were supposed to collect them. Finally, stricter supervision was also suggested of the customary system for allowances of beer to employees, whether there should be a voucher system "or whether cups ought not to be filled". He even considered stopping Christmas gifts of wine and spirits.

Some if not all of these strategies were put into operation in the following year. In March the travellers were interviewed and new schedules agreed, cutting out wasteful journeys, and the store at the Stratford Arms does seem to have been closed. Alban was also aware of the value of advertising in a competitive market. In 1904 a few years after the new brewery was completed, a poster was commissioned from E. S. and A. Robinson of Bristol with an artist's impression of the fine new buildings. The buildings were made to look as imposing as possible, sometimes at the expense of accuracy – in particular the tall chimney bears little resemblance to the two rather shorter ones that were actually there, and there are other details which are unlike the actual building. In the foreground is a large open space invented by the artist to allow him to depict a busy scene of horse-drawn drays and numerous brewery employees shifting casks in all directions. (A labour-intensive scene which might not have fitted in with Alban's economies had it existed in reality!) As in all advertising, it was the image rather than strict reality which mattered, and when a draft of the picture was sent to the directors for their approval, their only comments were to ask for the colour of the building to be improved so that it looked more like ironstone and less like red brick, for the shadow falling on the office entrance to be lightened so that the doorway with the name of the brewery could be seen more easily, and they asked the artist to add to the foreground scene of drays the company's new steam wagon which had just been delivered, and of which Alban was particularly proud. (The poster is still in use today, so the company has had good value from it, even if the building does still look rather more like brick than ironstone.) It was perhaps a large version of this poster which was to be used on the advertising board which the company erected in Bedford Street, Leamington, at a cost of £3 15s. Another was leased for £2 per year. Advertisements were also placed in the programmes of local horticultural shows and of the Chipping Norton Bazaar. This was no doubt intended to support these local organisations as well as to market beer, but it illustrates Alban's policy of promoting the company and maintaining goodwill.

He made conscious efforts to improve his skills in the management and administration of the company by studying articles in the trade journals. Pasted into the back of one of his brewing books is an index to articles in the *Brewer's Journal* on such topics as "The Office Department", "Management of Agencies" and "Sundry Accounts Ledgers". There is also a complicated algebraic formula for calculating beer duty, probably copied from the same source.

Improving the product: science or experience?

The *Brewer's Journal* was also useful for keeping up with the latest improvements in brewing methods. Most innovations were introduced by large firms like Bass with a national market, huge turnovers and resources to invest in R&D, but the Journal recognised the needs of small country brewers by printing articles about good practice and new methods and materials. At the end of the nineteenth century there was a debate about the role of chemistry in improving brewing methods, traditionalists denying that it could add anything to practical experience learned doing the job. A speaker at the annual dinner of the Midlands Institute of Brewing in 1897 delighted his audience by declaring that "They could not make a chemist in a brewery and they would not make a brewer in a laboratory" He had great faith in the practical brewer "because he was as scientific as many". The truth was that while a few of the largest breweries were beginning to employ chemists and to support the setting up of a university department to study the chemistry of brewing (eventually established at Birmingham close to the brewing capital of the world at Burton on Trent), small firms like Hook Norton which could not afford to do so, were still able to apply the results of such research without necessarily understanding the science behind them. They were indeed practical brewers, taking expert advice but relying on experience to show what worked best for their circumstances.

Although, rather surprisingly for a small brewery at such an early date, there was a room referred to as the laboratory next to the brewer's office at Hook Norton, the evidence in Alban Clarke's brewing books shows a good deal of trial and error when it came to judging the quantities of ingredients such as caramel used to improve the colour, or flaked maize or rice with the malt for mashing. The pages have frequent comments like "this was too much, try ½lb". There are also many references to chemicals being used to treat the liquor in order to give it the correct chemical constituency for different types of beer. The huge success of the Burton breweries in developing pale ale in the nineteenth century was based on the qualities of the "hard" water naturally available there, and it became the ambition of every brewer to imitate it in other parts of the country by chemical means. On the other hand, the "soft" water of the London region was particularly suited to brewing stout. Alban sought advice from a consultant brewer who advertised in the *Brewer's Journal*, and as a result of this advice was regularly adding substances like "Biosulphate of Lime" and "Kendall's Hardening" to pale ale brews, while he tried "Collett's Softening" when brewing Double and Single stout.

Much of the malt he used came from barley grown on their own farm and malted on site, but other varieties including foreign ones were combined with it. As many as seven kinds of hops were blended in some brews, with some being added about half an hour before turning out. Quite a lot of the yeast was purchased from Hitchman's Brewery in Chipping Norton, but yeast was also saved from his own brewing, and every now and then a special "all malt" brew using no other form of sugar was done specifically to produce a yeast culture. The beers being produced at this time included Double and Single Stouts, Mild and Pale Ale at various strengths denoted by the customary scale of "X" up to "XXXX". On one occasion he even tried a brew of cider, but the experiment was not repeated. Most of the beer was sold in casks (and conditioned with extra hops in the traditional way), but an increasing amount was bottled, partly to meet the growing demand for home consumption in this convenient form. The brewery also distributed wines and spirits.

Private trade at the turn of the century

John Harris & Co had built up an extensive private trade which was continued and developed by Alban and John Henry. Much correspondence passed between the brewery, the agents and individual customers, all laboriously handwritten and carbon copied by a patent method into volumes called "letter books" which still survive. They illustrate the costly nature of the private trade in time and money, which eventually lead to its abandonment after the First War, when severe economies had to be made in the operation of the business.

Meanwhile, in the early years of the century it was still an important feature of the company's trade, and no chance was missed to solicit potential customers, particularly well-to-do gentlemen like Gerald Trollope Esq, who received a letter from Alban Clarke offering to supply him with beer even before he had moved into his new home at Broughton Hall, Filkins. The letter mentions other highly respectable customers of the brewery as a recommendation, including Albert Brassey MP of Heythrop House and the Duke of Marlborough at Blenheim. Alban knew about Mr Trollope's forthcoming move to Filkins because he had been tipped off by his friend

Men and boys employed in the brewery in the early years of the twentieth century. Back row: Spatcher, P. Buggins, P. Randle, G. Beck, T. Cox, W. Coleman, T. Harris, G. Messer; Middle row: J. Gibbons, H. Busby, H. Haynes, Frank Beale (sen.), G. Matthews, W. Beck, G. Hall, Fred Beale, W. Gilkes; Front row: W. Hall, G. Horn, Frank Beale (jun.), C. Buggins, E. Savage, E. Embra, J. Pinfold

Mr Bloxham, builder of the new brewery, who was now working on repairs to Trollope's house in Filkins prior to his taking up residence. A farmer in Chipping Campden, who had sought a contribution from the brewery for a forthcoming livestock show, did not escape without a sales pitch: "We shall be glad to give a little assistance to the funds of the Campden Teg Show, and herewith send you 10s for the purpose. You will pardon us mentioning for your kind consideration that we intend opening wholesale stores in Campden during this month, for the purpose of supplying private families with our well known Malt Liquors". Such approaches were never pressed too far, however, and in guidance to a new and perhaps over zealous agent Alban wrote: "I think it would be better not to force Mr Burl to have our beer when he has not ordered it. No-one likes pressure put on and we make it a strict rule never to send goods unless definite orders have been received". He was equally fair in his dealings with rival breweries, refusing to supply the landlord of the Unicorn at Stow "as we make it an invariable rule not to supply the tenants of other brewing firms except for goods for which they are not tied".

Office staff c.1914. Back row: Frederick Stratford (Outride and later Empties Clerk); Middle row: Drake, Walker, Allen (Cashier); Front row: Frank Veale, Harold Wyton, E. Robbins, G. Groves (Secretary). Most were long-serving members of the brewery staff. Veale and Wyton both went on to become Company Secretary, and Wyton was eventually succeeded by Frederick Stratford's grandson in 1969.

Particularly respectful approaches were made to members of the clergy, several of whom were among the brewery's customers. The Rev Compton was written to as soon as he moved into the vicarage at Adderbury. "Hearing that you are in residence we take the liberty to solicit a share of your esteemed patronage. We supply the majority of the leading families in the neighbourhood including the Rev H. Jepp and Dr Robertson of Adderbury and the Rev Canon Teesdale of Bodicote". What the letter did not mention was that the Rev Canon Teesdale's account was somewhat overdue, and Alban had to send him a polite reminder: "We beg to remind you that our Mr Stratford will have the pleasure of waiting upon you tomorrow, Friday, and we should be very much obliged if you would favour us with a cheque". A rather sharper tone was adopted with another customer, probably of lower social standing, who owed the not inconsiderable sum of £7 15s. 8d. "We are surprised that you have allowed your account to remain up to the present unpaid, and we have now to say that Mr Stratford will call upon you on Wednesday next when payment must be made without fail."

Credit, sometimes for long periods, was a customary part of nearly all business dealings at this time and agents like Mr Stratford spent a good deal of their time trying to collect unpaid accounts. The gentry often would not, and poorer men could not, pay promptly and when other methods failed the company had to take them to court. In February 1911 at the Stratford magistrates court, Mr Toy presented cases on behalf of the company involving a farm worker who owed 12s. 6d., a schoolmaster £1 16s., and a roadman 6s. These seem quite small sums but they had all been owing for two or three years. the usual outcome of such cases was a small monthly payment. The company does seem to have been exceptionally lenient in some cases. A smallholder from Burmington owed £4 12s. 1d. in 1902 but was allowed to purchase a further 10 gallons of ale and stout the following year, and then 1½ bushels of malt and 1½lbs of hops for his own home brewing, making his total bill £5 13s 1d. In September 1904 he paid 4s. on account and sometime later Alban accepted 1 quarter of wheat and 3 bushels of potatoes as part payment in kind and agreed that the remainder could be paid off at 3s. per month.

Customers sometimes had cause to complain about the brewery, usually about bad beer. One of the hazards of the private trade was that beer did not travel very well, particularly in hot weather, and when this happened the firm had to replace it and apologise in order not to lose a valued client. Mr Fitz of Charlton Villas, Cheltenham, received such an apology in 1899 (using warm weather as a rather unlikey excuse in November). "We are very sorry to hear that the ale we have recently sent you has not been satisfactory. The weather as you know has been most trying and now the cooler weather has set in we shall be able to supply ale of the usual quality. Our Autumn brewed ales are now in splendid condition and if you will allow us to send you a cask of ale in exchange for the one you are returning we shall be happy to do so, as we shall be very sorry indeed to lose you as a customer."

"*Incurable stinkers*"

Another persistent hazard of the private trade was that the wooden casks in which the beer was supplied were often not returned promptly, and if they were left for any length of time the inside of the cask would become contaminated by the dregs of sour beer left in the bottom. Such casks were referred to in the trade as "stinkers", and in the worst cases the cask might become unusable, causing considerable loss to the brewery. It was the job of the agent to recover empty casks but the company was continually having to urge them to make greater efforts and it could become a serious problem. One of Alban Clarke's management resolutions in 1900 was to tighten up this aspect of the business. He wrote to an agent in 1901 "we have no district where there is so much neglect as in this, there being from 100 to 150 out up to last November. Where beer is sold and the cask spoilt the profit is nil – in fact it is trading at a loss." This explains the enormous lengths he sometimes went to in order to recover a single stray cask. He wrote to the former employer of a farm worker who had bought a cask of ale two years previously, asking for his present address or suggesting that the farmer might search his tied cottages in case the missing cask was still lying about. On another occasion he asked the Manager of the Great Western Railway Company goods

Poster commissioned in 1904 showing the new brewery

Old bottles and jars. The earthenware jars were used for spirits. Like wooden casks, each one was numbered so that its issue and return could be recorded

The brewery in 1999

The mash tun

The steam engine

The Pear Tree Inn, Hook Norton. This was the first tied house
purchased by John Harris in April 1869

Brewery staff in 1999

depot in Wolverhampton to send a cart to an address in the town to recover a single cask left in the front garden by a former customer who had now moved away: "The house is locked up but the key can be obtained from number 8."

The tied trade

"Stinkers" could occur in the tied trade too, but were less likely because of the much tighter control the brewery could exert over its tenants in all aspects of the trade. The great advantage of the tied house trade was that although there were expenses which the brewery had to meet, such as repairs and redecoration, it afforded guaranteed outlets and a higher profit margin than in free houses where large discounts had to be offered to induce landlords to sell one company's beer rather than their rival's. It was also much more cost effective in terms of the quantities supplied and sold at a single pub compared with the many small deliveries to scattered private addresses which characterised the private trade. Occasionally a tied house served also as a store, with the tenant being also agent for selling to private households in the area. The Coach and Horses in Banbury, where Mr Herring had an agency office in the 1900s, was an example of this.

The different financial arrangements for tied and free houses at this period are well illustrated by the contrast between the terms offered to the free landlord of the pub in Whichford in 1903, who was offered a discount of 25 per cent "hoping you will be able to increase your business with us", and the advertisement for a new tenant of the White Swan in Stratford on Avon which specified a rent of £60 and a mere 5 per cent discount on sales. These two figures for the tied tenant represent what was often referred to in the trade as "dry rent" and "wet rent", the wet rent being the higher price the tied tenant had to pay for his beer compared with the free house. This difference might have to be passed on to the customers by charging higher prices per pint, but there was a risk of losing trade by sending customers to drink in the cheaper free house instead. One way of keeping them was "the long pull" – filling the glass above the statutory pint mark. Generally, tied houses and their tenants did well, serving the interests of both tenant and company, but occasionally a tenant got into difficulties or proved unsuitable and Alban Clarke had the ultimate sanction of eviction in extreme cases.

An Edwardian "*local*"

Some impression of the inside of a small public house in the 1900s can be gleaned from details of its accommodation, fixtures and fittings listed for a change of tenancy in 1909. The Queen's Own at Woodstock took its name from the county's prestigious Yeomanry regiment, The Queen's Own Oxfordshire Hussars, which had close ties with the Churchill family at Bleheim Palace. It was a small pub which had been purchased by the brewery some time before 1898 and served a local clientele rather than the many visitors to Woodstock, who patronised the larger hotels and inns.

The public rooms consisted of a bar parlour, small taproom and "new" taproom linked by a passage which had shelves in a recess. There were presumably tables and wooden chairs in all these rooms and there were two settles against the walls in the new taproom. This room also had a deal double cupboard and was warmed by a "self setting range" with a fender in front of it. Some walls were papered, others distempered in a single colour, the woodwork painted, probably dark brown, and the ceilings "whitened". The lighting was by gas and there were gas brackets on the walls of all three rooms, those in the small taproom and the bar having incandescent burners to make them brighter. The old taproom was a rather dingy place with a simple flame from its gas lights and five spittoons on the floor. There were none elsewhere, suggesting that the habit was being restricted to one place. The bar had oil cloth and "lino" on the floor but in the other rooms there were just bare boards, probably spread with sawdust.

There was a fireplace in the bar with a mirror over the mantlepiece, and a blind at the window. On the bar was a "four-pull beer engine" (the device for pumping beer up from casks in the cellar, possibly requiring four pulls of the pump handle to produce one pint), and something else called a "removing engine". The pub was not a large one and the stock of glasses was limited to 25 pints,

12 half-pint "glass cups", 21 other unstamped glasses of various sizes and 5 soda water glasses. Beer could also be served in the six stamped quart jugs. In the cellar were three wooden cask stoops for supporting the barrels, again suggesting modest consumption. The pub sold Hook Norton ale and stout together with minerals, cigars and tobacco. For entertainment it provided its customers with a bagatelle board and two sets of dominoes.

The private accommodation for the tenant included a wash house with iron pan furnace (a "copper" for boiling clothes) and a chimney, a water tap and glazed sink. Rather surprisingly there was also a water tap in the coal house, and a water butt stood outside in the yard. Also outside was a toilet. The building was three storeys high and above the public rooms were front and back bedrooms on each floor for the family.

Extending the tied estate

The 1890s was a period when breweries all over the country were rushing to buy tied houses, and Hook Norton was part of this trend. Between 1890 and 1907 it acquired fourteen public houses and four beerhouses. Although there was clearly no intention of competing with the big "nationals" or even their main local rival, Hunt Edmunds of Banbury, their own estate spread over quite a wide area, including pubs like The Black Horse in Leamington, The Kettle in Chipping Campden, The George Hotel in Shipston on Stour and both the Reindeer and the Coach and Horses in Banbury. There were others in Chipping Norton, Stratford and Stow as well as many villages in between.

A new man at the top

With so much competition for houses nationally and locally it was inevitable that prices would rise and there was a real danger of a brewery overstretching its resources. This was possibly the experience of the Hook Norton Company, and might explain the change in management which happened in 1913. The expenditure on property between 1890 and 1907 amounted to £22,813 which included not only the tied houses but several cottages, a butchers shop and some land in Hook Norton itself. Several of the purchases were achieved with mortgages, reducing the amount of capital to be found immediately but increasing the company's long term liabilities. When it is considered that the brewery was completely rebuilt and equipped at a cost of a further £20,000 during the same period and that sales and profits declined steadily after 1907, it is likely that the company was facing difficulties by 1913 in spite of all Alban Clarke's efforts. This may explain the decision by the directors to bring an outsider onto the board, with fresh ideas and enthusiasm. Alban was 55 in 1913 and had spent most of his life in the brewery, carrying the responsibility of managing director for more than two decades; perhaps he wanted to shed some of the responsibility and get back to the pleasures of practical brewing.

Whatever the reason, and it is not fully explained in the surviving records, in 1913 Percy William Flick, a Banbury estate agent, took over as Managing Director of the company. Alban resigned that position and became a working director in charge of the brewing operation while John Henry gave up all his working responsibilities and became merely an ordinary director, although he leased the farm from the company and ran that. William Toy remained Chairman. New service agreements were drawn up confirming the changes. Percy Flick eventually became the largest preference shareholder and was to guide the company through the difficult years of the First World War and beyond.

The death of Alban Clarke

On a Saturday afternoon in March 1917, Alban set off on one of his usual fishing trips cycling down to Traitor's Ford, a well known local spot a few miles from Hook Norton on the road to Sibford. He had planned the outing earlier in the day and arranged with one of the brewery men to carry his fishing basket to the ford so that he could follow on his bicycle. It was not his own cycle as that was being repaired, but one he had borrowed for the day. Alban never arrived at the chosen spot. Later that afternoon he was found on the steep hill down to Temple Mill, lying in the road with blood pouring from his badly cut head, only half conscious and unable to move or speak. Some hours later he was eventually brought back to Hook Norton and examined by a doctor, but died later that evening. His death was a huge shock not only to the family but to everyone at the brewery which had been such a big part of his life. The whole village mourned his passing and many of them joined the procession following his coffin, carried by six brewery workers, from the church to the village cemetery.

4
STEAM POWER IN THE BREWERY

PERHAPS the most remarkable survival at the Hook Norton brewery is the 25hp steam engine which still drives all the machinery used in the brewery just as it has done for the past hundred years. Installed in 1899, it is believed to be the last steam engine in the country still in daily use for its original purpose. It is not a museum exhibit, but the driving force behind all the main brewing processes. The brewery today depends entirely on this engine just as it always has done – when it stops, the brewery stops.

The earliest engine

John Harris had an earlier steam engine installed in his brewery, probably in 1880 but little is known about it. It was used to pump the liquor, to drive a grist mill and for hoisting sacks and barrels. A rough plan of this brewery in the 1880s shows its position and various belt drives running from it. When the new brewery was built at the turn of the century the accounts include "thoroughly overhauling and fixing the present engine and barrel hoist for loading-out stage, including additions and alterations to shafting and gearing for same", suggesting that it continued to have a limited use for some time even though the new engine had taken over the main role.

The Buxton & Thornley steam engine, 1899

The engine in use today was supplied by Buxton & Thornley Ltd of Burton on Trent on October 18th, 1899, at a cost of £175. It is a 25hp engine with a single horizontal cylinder.

TECHNICAL DETAILS

    Steam pressure: 80 psi.

    Cylinder: 10" dia, 22" stroke, overhung.

    Valves: Thornley drop inlet, Corliss exhaust, driven by two eccentrics.

    Crank: Disc, counterbalanced.

    Flywheel: 7' diameter, 9" face.

    Belt pulleys: 4' and 18" (All drives are now via belt and lineshaft from the larger pulley).

An unusual feature of this engine is that it is fitted with a type of valve cut-off gear invented by Mr George Thornley, one of the partners in the firm of Buxton & Thornley. The mechanism was later described in detail in *Engineering* vol. LXXVIII, 1904. A reciprocating rod passes through loops in the drop valve spindles. The valves at each end of the cylinder are opened in sequence by conical ends of the rod and then sharply closed by a trip falling into a spiral groove in these conical ends. The precise position of the groove, and thus the timing of the valve closure, is controlled by slight rotation of the rod produced by a quadrant and pinion moving with the action of the governor. As the engine gathers speed the arms on the governor rise, moving the pinion to turn the reciprocating rod, which in turn causes the valves to close earlier. The effect is thus to regulate the speed of the engine keeping it constant whatever the load.

Steam Power in the Brewery

The Buxton and Thornley 25HP steam engine, installed in 1899 and still in daily use a century later

Detail of the Thornley patent valve mechanism

The boilers

In the 1970s two disused boilers were recorded at the brewery: a Cornish type, supplied by Barrows & Co of Banbury and dated 1891, and a Lancashire type. These were probably the original boilers for the two steam engines. Both were coal fired, and this system remained in use until the 1970s. Michael Turnock remembers being employed with his father during the holiday week at the brewery when the engine was stopped, to climb inside the boiler and remove all the soot and ash which had built up around the flues before its annual inspection. A variety of coal seems to have been in use, including steam coal, nutty slack, anthracite and some coke. On an occasion in the early 1900s, Alban Clarke, who always had an eye for economy, discovered that the boiler would burn the "screened cobbles" which had been in use for the previous year in the filters through which all the brewery waste passed before it entered the stream. When the filters were being renewed he was delighted to find that he could save some money, and wrote to the coal merchant in Banbury postponing further deliveries until this unexpected source had been used up.

Plant driven by the steam engine

The steam engine drives a range of machinery in the brewery via belts and line shafting.

PUMPS: The brewery's precious water supply comes from wells on the site. It is pumped up to the top of the brewery at the start of the process. A further pumping operation takes place after the hops have been added when the boiled wort is again taken up to the cooling plant under the roof to reduce the temperature before fermentation. All this pumping is achieved by the original Buxton and Thornley pumps.

MASHING: The Steele's Masher (patented in 1853) and the rake which slowly stirs the grains in the liquor, are connected to the line-shafting.

Steam Power in the Brewery

A pair of gear wheels in the overhead line shaft, showing the wooden teeth used in one of the wheels.

One of the pumps for raising water from the wells to the top of the building.

Grist mill made by Nalder and Nalder of Wantage in 1899

BARREL LIFT: After filling with beer the barrels are lowered from the ground floor down to the cellar in the 1900 Waygood's lift, also powered by overhead lineshafting.

SACK HOIST: This takes the sacks of malt from the delivery lorry up to the second floor store.

GRIST MILL: On the top floor of the first stage is a grist mill for crushing the malt so that it can release its sugar in the mashing process. Supplied in 1900 by Nalder and Nalder of Wantage, this is another example of original machinery which is still in use, and it may be the last one of its kind.

Overhead line shafting

A particularly interesting detail of the mechanism is that in each pair of gearwheels in the overhead drive system one wheel has wooden teeth while the other has iron. This simple engineering strategy means that if there is ever a sudden jamming of the drive, the only result will be damage to a few wooden teeth which can easily be replaced, instead of a whole casting being ruined. The same advantage confines everyday wear mainly to the wooden teeth, which normally last for about ten years. They are still made of hornbeam, the traditional timber used for this purpose because it is durable without being too hard. New teeth are shaped and fitted by the brewery's own engineer.

Steam heating

The copper in which the wort is boiled was heated directly by a coal fire until the 1970s when steam pipes were inserted to do the work rather more efficiently.

Steam also helped to maintain the efficiency of the staff, by supplying a heating system to the new office building when it was completed in 1897.

Cask washing required ample supplies of hot water which was heated by re-using the exhaust steam from the engine. A note in the brewing book for 1901 records that the temperature of water in the washing tank was raised by this means from 74°F at 8.0 am to 180° by 3.30 pm. Modern metal casks are still washed using water heated in this way.

5

PERCY FLICK

Survival between the wars

WHEN Percy Flick became the Managing Director of the Hook Norton Brewery Company in 1913, he brought to the firm professional expertise which was to be very significant. Fourteen years earlier he had set himself up as an auctioneer and estate agent in Banbury and was now well established and widely respected in the town and surrounding area. Born in 1873 at Halesworth in Suffolk, the son of Richard and Charlotte Flick, he came to Banbury as a boy when the family moved there in the late 1880s. His father described himself as a brewer and wine and spirit merchant and in 1889 was licensee of The Flying Horse in Parson's Street Banbury. Here he ran the "Horseshoe Brewery" and was a member the Country Brewers Society. Publicans who brewed their own beer had once been common but were now fast declining as larger breweries proved more efficient. Richard Flick seems to have done reasonably well, however, and the family could afford to employ a cook and a housemaid. At least two of his sons were given some early experience in the trade – George, as a brewer's assistant, and Percy as assistant to a maltster. So Percy was no stranger to brewing when he

Percy William Flick, 1873–1951

came to Hook Norton, and he later married into another brewing family, the Thornleys, who had a brewery at Radford Semele near Leamington.

He made use of his brewing background when setting up as an estate agent, advertising in 1900 as an "Expert licensed victuallers' valuer and public house broker". He had by this time taken over the licence of The Flying Horse himself. It was one of Banbury's older inns, having survived the fire which destroyed much of the town in 1628 and the Civil War which destroyed even more a few years later.

PERCY W. FLICK,

Auctioneer, Valuer,

LAND, HOUSE, & INSURANCE AGENT,

PUBLIC HOUSE BROKER.

Expert Licensed Victuallers' Valuer.

OFFICES:

44, Parson's Street, BANBURY.

Weekly Sales (on Thursdays,) of Agricultural and Dairy Produce, Fruit, Vegetables, Pigs and Poultry, are held in the Flying Horse Sale Yard.

SALES BY AUCTION AND VALUATIONS MADE FOR ALL PURPOSES.

Percy Flick's advertisement in Pott's Banbury Directory for 1900. He is described as an auctioneer and valuer specialising in licensed property. (Banbury Library, Local History Collection)

It was a lively place in the nineteenth century with its own bowling green for entertainment (though modern bowlers who require near perfect grass surfaces would be horrified to hear that in 1847 a large horticultural show was staged on this green attended by 800 people!). In the yard at the rear of the pub Percy ran sales of pigs, poultry, agricultural and dairy produce, fruit and vegetables. It is interesting that the landlord almost a hundred years later in 1995 decided to change the name of this pub renaming it Ye Olde

Auctioneer, a quite inaccurate form of spelling for the Victorian period, but clearly intended to commemorate Percy Flick.

Alban Clarke and John Henry Harris had perhaps already had dealings with Percy Flick as an estate agent. William Toy the Chipping Norton Solicitor who acted for the company and became Chairman of the Directors would also have known of him and may have been instrumental in recruiting him for the Company. His background and track record made him eminently suitable for the task. He knew his value, and negotiated a salary of £500 plus expenses and an annual bonus equal to the total dividend paid to the family for their ordinary shares. His contract was to spend at least two days per week working for the brewery, as he was still running his own estate agents firm in Banbury. Together, Flick and Toy guided the brewery through the difficult period during and after the First World War, and it fell to Flick to take up the reins after the tragic death of Alban Clarke. It was undoubtedly his careful management and husbanding of resources which ensured the survival of the firm through the twenties and thirties when many other small breweries were swallowed up by larger firms. By 1940 there were less than half the number of brewing firms in the country that there had been in 1920, but the Hook Norton Brewery was still independent and the next generation of the Clarke family was being trained up to take over.

A brewery at war

Little more than a year after Percy Flick took over as Managing Director, the First World War broke out and the brewing industry was faced with all kinds of new problems which affected large and small breweries alike. The first was a huge increase in taxation, in order to raise much needed revenue for the government towards the cost of the war. The amount of duty per standard barrel of beer rose from 7s. 9d. to £1 3s. in November 1914, and by 1918 had reached £2 10s.

More controversial was the Government's policy of restricting output by the brewers and consumption by their customers. This policy was motivated partly by the requirements of the wartime economy and the need to conserve energy and raw materials for other purposes, but was also inspired by the Temperance movement which had a strong lobby in Parliament at this time. Lloyd George was himself a supporter of the movement and inclined to listen to its arguments. In the desperate rush to manufacture armaments and munitions it was alleged that output was being held back by the heavy drinking habits of factory workers, and so the opening times of licensed premises, especially during the working day, were drastically reduced. This measure cut opening hours from about 16 hours a day to 5½ hours on weekdays and 5 on Sundays, with a compulsory closure in the afternoon. In 1916 the government also put a limit on the amount of beer any brewery could produce, reducing the supply to the pubs. This was justified on grounds of conserving energy and raw materials for the war effort, but was also fuelled by temperance zeal. It is not surprising that neither of these measures was at all popular with the majority of the working population and some concessions were eventually made in the interests of keeping the workforce happy. These included allowing more beer to be brewed, but requiring it to be of a lower specific gravity (1036°). Such weak beer became known derisively as "government ale".

There was some decline in sales from Hook Norton in the autumn of 1915 but this was attributed to a spell of bad weather and the closure of one of the outstores from which private customers in the Witney area were supplied. Flick had given instructions to the brewery's agents that they were not to take orders on credit from customers who might have difficulty paying their bills "in the present unsettled times" and this probably contributed to the downturn.

Patriotism was high at the beginning of the war, and when the customers of the Black Horse in Leamington invited Percy Flick to become President of their recently formed Air Gun Club he readily accepted, adding that:

> At no time has it been more imperative that Shooting Clubs should be fostered . . . . At the same time, if your members can see their way to start a Subscription List, the proceeds to be devoted either to the Local Fund or the Prince of Wales' Fund

for the Relief of Suffering caused by this disastrous war, we shall be glad to consider it our duty to assist you.

Later in the war the brewery sent a contribution of £26 5s. to the British Brewers' Ambulance Convoy.

In September 1915 Dunnell's Brewery in North Bar Banbury was in trouble and Alban Clarke asked whether Hook Norton should take them over. The directors decided against this, but said they might be willing to purchase some of their tied houses in the Hook Norton area. Flick's experience would no doubt be useful in assessing the value of these and getting them at the right price, and in January 1916 the formidable team of Flick the estate agent and Toy the solicitor forced the Warwick Licensing Authority to agree generous compensation of £660 for the closure of The Blue Pig at Southam. The unlicensed property was then sold at auction by Flick for £290. Magistrates had the power to refuse licences and if the bench was inclined towards Temperance, might do so on the slightest provocation simply to reduce the number of drinking places in the area. It was therefore important to show that the company's houses were orderly and well managed, and when there was a disturbance at The Reindeer Inn in Banbury one night it was felt expedient "because of the proximity of the licensing meeting" to give the landlord notice. Fortunately the magistrates renewed the license without comment and the company withdrew the notice, the landlord merely receiving a strong warning.

The restrictions on brewing and the shortening of opening hours did not have too much effect on Hook Norton at first, rural areas being less affected than larger towns, indeed the employees were given a rise of 1s per week for boys and up to 2s. for men, with an appropriate increase for the staff in the office, and later in the year for the directors themselves. This was described as a War Bonus "in view of the increased cost of living". However, at the end of 1915 a considerable fall-off in sales was noticed, and although they picked up temporarily in the autumn of 1916, the overall picture was worrying. Government restrictions were beginning to bite and the usual beer-drinking population was being reduced as men left the district either to join the forces or to work in munitions and other heavy industries in the Midlands. The new Liquor Control Regulations meant that the brewery's Agent in the Stratford on Avon area was prevented from canvassing for orders, and Flick told his fellow directors that he "could hold out no hope of securing any additional trade". In 1916 all the company's properties were insured against aircraft damage.

The workforce at the brewery was also reduced as men volunteered for the army, or were called up when conscription started in 1916. Before the outbreak of war in 1914, there had been 30 men and boys working in the brewery and stables (the base for the draymen). By April 1915 this was down to 26, and throughout the rest of the war it steadily declined, until at the end of 1918 only 8 men and 2 boys were employed. There was some confusion over the call-up system at first — W. Wyatt was given a send-off when he left in March 1916, only to return two days later "because of a mistake in

Harold Wyton in uniform during the First World War. He had gone to work at the brewery straight from school in 1909. He joined the army in 1916, was badly wounded, losing his left arm, and returned to the brewery after the war, remaining there for the rest of his working life

his Group". He remained at the brewery until August before again being called up. In June three other men went – J. Pinfold, E. Pinfold and W. Beale, and the company made them a gift of 10s., which then became the custom each time a man was called up.

The office staff was also depleted. Frank Veale, who had joined the company in 1899, went into the army in March 1916 and in July Harold Wyton followed him. He had joined the brewery straight from the village school in 1909, starting work in the stables but quickly being promoted to the office. After basic training at several camps in England he was sent to France where he celebrated his 21st birthday in July 1916. The following February he was severely wounded, lost his left arm, and returned to England. Recovering at an army hospital he received a letter from Percy Flick which shows real concern and pride in all the former employees "who are standing between us at home and destruction":

> I am sending your brother Walter down to see you as soon as we know it will be possible for him to do so, and after that I should, if I may, like to run down and see you myself.
> I had E. Pinfold, P. Buggins and Alcock home on leave for a few days some month or so ago. They were all well, and I have safe news of W. Cross in Salonika, F. Veale, Robins and Matthews are all safe and well.
> With kindest wishes from the "old Boys" of the Staff and myself, and trusting we may soon welcome you among us.

Both Frank Veale and Harold Wyton were indeed welcomed back after the war, and continued in the office for the rest of their working lives. Veale completed fifty years service in 1949 and Wyton, by now Company Secretary, finally retired in 1969 after 60 years with the firm.

Meanwhile, others were still leaving the brewery to join the forces, among them key men like Herbert Matthews the cooper who repaired the casks and kept them serviceable. This was very skilled work and impossible to replace except by the efforts of men who had seen him at work and had a rough idea of what was required. Fortunately, the reduced output of beer meant that fewer casks were needed, and so they were able to get by. At one point surplus casks were even sold off to raise a bit of much needed revenue in the worst period. Bert Matthews returned to work after his war service and was another who completed 50 years.

As more of the employees were called up it was agreed that the remaining men would take on their work if necessary and share the wages between them, but there was a limit to the amount of extra work they could do. In 1916 they missed their usual Bank Holiday at the beginning of August because of the pressure of work, and were given a day off in September instead. Other novel measures had to be taken that summer to keep production going and it must have caused a considerable stir when the first women came to work in the brewery – a development which was happening in industries all over the country. It seems that "Girl Clerks" were taken on in the office, but Minnie Hall and Mary Cross started in the brewery itself in June 1916 at a wage of 2s. a day, just over half the average rate for men. They were joined a week later by May Harris and their pay went up to 2s. 3d. a day, giving them 13s. 6d. for a 50 hour week. In that busy August they worked overtime and all day on Saturday like the men.

However, this level of work was not to last, and sales began to show a serious decline in the winter months. By February 1917 figures for the last four months showed a drop of about £500 and the government's latest restrictions on output were due to take effect in April, threatening to depress profits even further. Then there were individual events like the call-up of the tenant of The Queen's Own at Woodstock, whose wife after struggling to keep the pub going while her husband was serving in France had finally locked up and left, meaning the complete loss of trade until a new tenant could be found. The real problem, however, was the general change in trading conditions due to the war. Practices which had succeeded before the war were no longer appropriate, and this was particularly true of the Private Trade, the inefficiencies of which were becoming obvious. "The Company had been endeavouring to preserve its Goodwill by undertaking journeys which neither paid the cost of travelling or delivery". Very drastic measures would have to be taken immediately and Flick estimated that a cut of at least 50% would have to be made in running costs. Even the possibility of amalgamation with another brewery was considered.

As trade was now so limited three long-standing Agents became redundant, including Mr Stratford one of the original "outrides". The directors, showing how unhappy they were to have to do this to a faithful employee found him work in the office at a much reduced salary as Empties Clerk checking on the return of empty casks. Among the office staff "the lately employed Girl Clerks" were discharged (though a Miss Tyrrell is mentioned the next year, so perhaps she survived) and even Mr Allen the Cashier was warned that he might have to go if things did not improve. In the brewery the three women and some boys were quickly laid off, leaving only six men and two boys with four draymen. In May brewing of stout was stopped because sales had fallen particularly badly, although Guiness was bottled and distributed from Hook Norton. Full barrels were shipped from Dublin to their agency in Bristol and from there to other breweries together with Guiness labels for the bottles.

At this low point in the Company's trading history, it suffered the greatest loss of all in the sudden death of Alban Clarke who apart from everything else was in charge of the brewing, on which the reputation of the whole operation depended.

The club trade

A regime of stringent economy continued under Percy Flick, indeed his reluctance to spend money that was not absolutely essential was one of the features most people remember about him. In November 1917 there was a shortage of oil and candles for lighting the brewery (or perhaps just a wish to keep the costs down) and so rather than go to extra expense it was arranged that the men's hours should be altered to make use of the daylight "except on brewing days". Even as late as 1928 Flick rejected the idea of installing electric lighting in the brewery as "a needless expense, and not at all necessary"! Two draymen had to pay 3s. to be allowed some of the manure from the stables for their gardens. Such carefulness may seem excessive today but it was one factor in Percy Flick's survival strategy for the brewery during the difficult war years. The other was his success in winning contracts to supply beer to several Working Men's Clubs in the Coventry area.

When Lloyd George's government restricted the availability of beer at the beginning of the war, one of its declared motives was to increase production of more essential goods, but it had the inevitable consequence of antagonising sections of the workforce whose cooperation it needed. In the long run industrial unrest was more damaging to the war effort than beer, and so the restrictions were partially relaxed to allow additional supplies of beer in those areas where munitions were being manufactured. Some time in 1917 or 1918 Percy Flick was successful in winning a contract to supply beer from Hook Norton to Working Men's Clubs serving factories in Coventry. He did so under special government licence permitting him "to supply beer in excess of the limits prescribed by the Intoxicating Liquor Order 1917". It was his most important and lasting contribution to the brewery and undoubtedly vital to its survival not only during the war, but throughout the even more difficult inter-war years. In 1918 no less than ten clubs were being supplied. They included the Coventry Working Men's Club and the Vauxhall Club (the two largest) together with the Amalgamated Engineers, Workers' Union, Constitutional, Stoke and the West End Club in Spon Street, as well as others. The Special Licence system applied to other essential industries as well, and extra supplies were authorised for the Red Lion at Long Compton "when the timber workers were in that area". The extra production brought by these arrangements was a lifeline to the brewery at a time when normal sales were restricted.

Other factors also helped. To the surprise of many brewery directors the government restrictions turned out not to be so damaging as they had expected. Greater efficiency of production was achieved as staffing levels were reduced and the lower gravity beer was cheaper to produce. At Hook Norton production was as high as possible in the circumstances and profits improved at the close of the war. Special bonuses were paid to employees, staff and directors at the end of 1918, several mortgages on brewery property were redeemed, some unprofitable tied houses sold, and even the Company's auditors were paid an extra 2 guineas on their annual fee.

Between the wars

The end of the war brought few of the improvements in the trade which had been hoped for and the 1920s and 30s were a very difficult period. Government restrictions on output were removed but the wartime limits on pub opening hours remained with only slight modification. These were hard years in many industries, with widespread unemployment and low wages. In Hook Norton itself the Brymbo Ironworks, involved in ironstone mining and processing at the other end of the village from the brewery and a major employer of local labour, cut its production and laid off many men, not returning to full production until the Second World War.

There was a short period of optimism at the brewery for the first few years. The staff which had been reduced to a minimum during the war, was increased as two or three former employees returned. By 1920 the labour force consisted of six men and a boy in the brewery, four draymen and two boys in the stables, plus the cooper. This was still much lower than pre-war. There were also about five office staff, including the Secretary, Cashier, Empties Clerk, and other clerical staff. Wages, which had risen during the war with bonuses and extra work, again increased sharply between February 1919 and May 1920. The two highest paid men in the brewery and stables in 1915 had earned 22s. By 1918 this had risen to 31s. 6d., and at the end of 1920 they were receiving 45s. Pay for the other men rose proportionally. Matthews the cooper, always paid more than the others in recognition of his skills, was earning 53s. 6d. a week in 1920. Boys starting work at 14 were paid 9s. a week, increasing with age to 30s. at 20, before going onto a man's wage at 21. Hours of work varied from summer to winter, the men doing 50 hours in summer and 48 in the winter months.

In 1922 the situation changed and the post-war depression set in. In January the wages were cut by 3s. for men and 1s. for boys, and a further cut of 5% came two weeks later reducing the top rate to 40s. It stayed at this level throughout the rest of the 1920s and 1930s, only rising again in 1940 when another war was in progress.

The end of private trade

In the harsh circumstances of the inter-war years some breweries expanded considerably seeking economies of scale, while others strove to maintain a local market and to keep costs as low as possible. As early as 1919 Percy Flick had recognised the altered conditions of the market and announced his policy for survival to his fellow directors: "to preserve what wholesale trade was possible, and only as a last resort to attempt to reconstruct the old style of Private Trade."

For more than half a century the mainstay of the brewery's success had been the Private Trade, selling direct to individual customers buying beer for home consumption and to free houses. Such trade depended on goodwill and required the maintenance of outlying depots and stores run by Agents who received a commission on sales as well as their salary. It also involved much travelling by the Agents to canvass orders or to collect payments which were frequently overdue, as well as inefficient journeys by the brewery's drays to deliver small uneconomic loads to private customers. Bad debts accumulated because Agents on commission were reluctant to turn

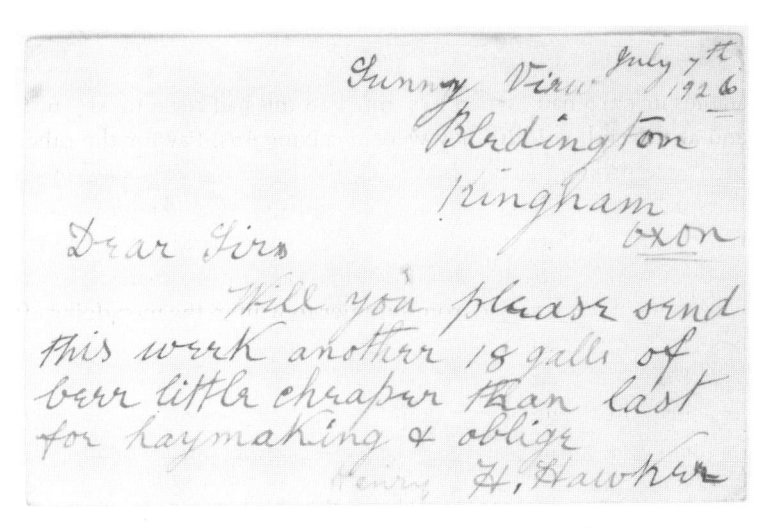

Postcard order for harvest beer from a farmer in 1923

down an order, and all business was done on credit. This resulted in endless court cases to recover small sums, which cost staff time and solicitor's fees. The likelihood of casks being lost or not being returned before they became what the trade called "stinkers", was also much greater with this kind of trade. In the pre-war days when trade was generally good the inefficiencies of the private trade had not seemed to matter too much and it was accepted as the traditional way for a small brewery to do business. The disruption caused by the war, however, the decline in consumption of beer, and rising labour and transport costs, had created a new climate in which running costs had to be reduced, all of which pointed to the greater efficiency of the tied trade with an "estate" of guaranteed outlets. To increase the Company's holding of public houses in the local area became one arm of the survival strategy in these years.

The tied estate

Flick's expertise as an estate agent (he was still an active partner in the Banbury firm of Flick & Lock which he had founded) was particularly important in valuing and purchasing new public houses for the Company. When in 1925 another local brewery, Blencowe's, was selling up, he produced his own expert valuation and an estimate of what each of their houses was likely to fetch at auction, and five were subsequently bought for a total of £3,175. These were very cheap purchases, other houses costing considerably more. £2,000 was paid for the Three Conies in Thorpe Mandeville in 1920 and two years later he was prepared to bid up to £3,300 for the Tower Inn at Edgehill (now The Castle). In a declining market breweries all over the country were rushing to buy up properties, and prices were inevitably pushed up. In 1929 Flick was particularly anxious to buy The New Inn at Whichford which was coming up for auction with a close of land attached. After much discussion it was agreed that he should bid up to £1,600 but he could use his discretion to go higher "it being recognised that the trade of the house was of vital importance to the Company". Others were also interested in it and Flick had to pay £2,100 to acquire it, considerably more than they had hoped. At the same time other houses were being sold, presumably because they were unprofitable or because the Company wished to concentrate its estate in a smaller area to reduce transport costs. Pubs in Stratford on Avon and Rowington were among these.

Steps were also taken to promote the profitability of existing houses. A donation of £21 from the Hook Norton Brewery to the Banbury Market Defence Committee "in an endeavour to retain the market in the centre of the town as heretofor", was clearly prompted by self interest rather than mere generosity, as the trade of two of the Company's houses in Banbury, the Reindeer and the Coach and Horses, would be affected if it moved. Markets were always good for business, and a particularly astute deal was done over a piece of land attached to the Red Lion in Cattle Market, Chipping Norton, which the Chipping Norton Borough Council wanted to lease for use on market days. When first approached in 1923, the directors of the brewery refused, but further consideration of the possible advantages to the trade of the Red Lion made them reconsider. Perhaps their Chairman, William Toy the Chipping Norton Solicitor and former Mayor, got wind that the Council were thinking of buying an adjoining bit of land as well, and so Flick moved quickly, bought this piece for the brewery "to ensure the control of the whole Sale Yard as an adjunct to the Red Lion", and then leased it to the Council.

While tied houses were a good investment, they did need money spending to maintain them in a good state of repair and decoration. There seems to have been no shortage of capital for buying them but finding the money for repairs was always more difficult, on one occasion Flick himself lending the company £2,000. Due to his extreme caution the work was frequently postponed. Tenders for repair work from local builders were never accepted without bargaining and the price was usually forced down. Things were so bad in 1928 that no less than 22 buildings including the brewery itself were in urgent need of repairs, but only 7 could be dealt with "as soon as the state of the finances permits".

These were indeed difficult times and all Percy Flick's care over unnecessary spending was essential to keep the Company's head above water. In the early 1930s there was a considerable fall-off in sales and profits dropped. The Ordinary Share dividends were reduced for several years, and none was paid at all in 1933 or 1934. Even the customary Christmas bonus for the office staff was discontinued for a time.

The club trade undoubtedly helped the Company through this difficult period. Percy Flick worked hard to develop it, and new clubs in Rugby as well as Coventry became good customers of the Hook Norton Brewery. He cultivated the goodwill and loyalty of the management committees, making regular personal visits to the clubs, the Company having met half the cost of a motor car which allowed him to do this, and on at least one occasion holding a huge garden party in the grounds of his house at Brailes for club members. A band played and the members showed their appreciation by giving special presents to Percy's daughters. (One of them still possesses a large Teddy bear from this occasion.) The brewery donated trophies and prizes for club events and considered the expense well justified even in a time of such stringency, recognizing that the club trade accounted for nearly a quarter of the Company's business. This also made them willing to lend quite large sums for the enlargement and improvement of club facilities. The Vauxhall Club, Binley Colliery Club and the Coventry Toolmakers' Club were among those who benefited in this way, but there was also a considerable benefit to the brewery in ensuring good outlets for their beer as well as receiving interest on the loans.

The family connection

As Managing Director Percy Flick was the driving force behind the Company throughout this period, providing invaluable expertise and leadership. Later on, as one of his economies, he took over the work of Secretary as well to avoid having to pay someone else when George Groves died, but there was no time when his fellow directors did not also include a member of the founding family. When Alban Clarke died the other directors were William Toy and John Henry Harris, who had resigned from his post in the brewery at the time Flick was appointed, but still remained on the board as a major shareholder. Perhaps he had been reluctant to accept someone from outside the family as Managing Director, and there are hints of disagreement between these two from time to time over some of Flick's policies.

William Toy died in May 1924 and was succeeded on the board by Frances Elizabeth Clarke, Alban's widow, thus strengthening the family representation. John Henry became Chairman, and they were sometimes prepared to outvote Flick, such as the occasion when they forced through the decision to purchase the first motor lorry in 1929, an expense which Flick had opposed (although, typically, he had already used the possibility of having to buy a lorry as an excuse to save money by cutting down on the repair of horse-drawn drays). For most of the time, however, there seems to have been harmony among the directors. John Henry Harris died in 1934 and was succeeded on the board by Frances and Alban Clarke's son William, who had already been working in the brewery for six years and was destined eventually to become Managing Director, as the third generation of the family to head the firm. Meanwhile, his mother was elected Chairman and held that position until her resignation in 1939, continuing as director until her death in 1943, when she was succeeded by Bill Clarke's sisters Frances and Nancy. The family involvement therefore was continuous, and although the long period in the brewery's history from 1915 to 1951 is very much the Percy Flick era, the Company remained firmly and ultimately in the control of the family because of their holding of almost all of its ordinary shares. Under Bill Clarke they would also resume the family's direct involvement in the brewing operation, which continues to the present day.

Village families

There were other families in Hook Norton, apart from the owners, who had long-standing associations with the brewery and it was not unusual for sons to follow fathers in working there. Sometimes there were several members of a family employed at the same time. The Beale family in particular was an example of this in the first part of the twentieth century, Frank Beale and Fred Beale both starting work in the 1890s and eventually becoming the highest paid men, Frank in the brewery and Fred in the malthouse. Alban Clarke relied on their experience, skill and loyalty, and both continued to work in Percy Flick's time, Frank finally retiring in 1933 and Fred a year later. Other relatives also worked there and in 1910 there were no less than six Beales employed: Frank, Fred, F. Beale junior (in the office), Walter, Arthur, and William. In 1921 Albert Beale joined the brewery straight from school shortly before his 14th birthday and worked until 1939.

Several employees worked for very long periods with the firm, Harold Wyton probably being the longest at 60 years. George Groves, first Company Secretary, died in office after 56 years service, Frank Veale and Mr Stratford both completed 50 years. These were office staff, and in the brewery itself, apart from the Beales there were Matthews the cooper and John Hall a drayman who were also long-serving men. The Company recognised the loyalty of such men, and although it rejected the idea of introducing a company pension scheme, on a number of occasions it did in fact give a small pension to a long-serving employee, or a single "gratuity" to their widow. In one case this took the form of a weekly credit of 7s 6d for groceries at the village shop.

Another war and the end of an era

The Second World War did not bring the same degree of difficulty to the brewing industry as the First had. There was no direct policy of restricting output in the way that Lloyd George's government had done and although there were other restrictions affecting the trade indirectly, national production of beer (measured in standard barrels) increased by about 15 per cent between 1938 and 1945.

This was in spite of periodic shortages of labour and of most raw materials, including wood for casks. Flaked maize and oats were tried as substitutes for barley. There were restrictions on the use of fuel and transport, but these probably had less effect on local distribution by small breweries like Hook Norton than on large companies with national distribution networks. All were affected by the order reducing the standard gravity of beer, intended to restrict the use of energy and raw materials, and by the inevitable huge increase in taxation to provide more revenue for the war effort – a trend which continued after the war was over. In spite of all this pre-tax profits for most breweries "soared" according to one authority and at Hook Norton there was certainly a recovery from the depression of the pre-war years. Ordinary share dividends made a modest improvement when the war started and were at their highest level for many years in 1943 to 1945. Bonuses for the staff were also restored.

As in the First War, women again helped the brewery to survive by filling gaps in the labour force and undertaking work previously done by men. Not only were men called up for the forces, but the Brymbo ironworks went back into full production because of the wartime demand for steel, and this meant that fewer men were available locally for work at the brewery. Mrs Heritage and Mrs Dumbleton were taken on as part-timers in the winter of 1942 and were joined two years later by Mrs King and Mrs Marshall. By this time Mrs Dumbleton was working full-time and was being paid a wage comparable to the men's. After the war, however, the men's wages increased at a higher rate so that a considerable differential developed. Mrs Dumbleton remained at the brewery until 1960. Other women were employed, mainly part-time, on a regular basis from the 1950s.

One unusual effect of the war which is still remembered in the village was the billeting of soldiers at the brewery. Among several units housed here while in transit were men of the Durham Light Infantry who occupied the former stable building as well as a camp constructed in the field behind the brewery. Stories were told that they had been sent to protect the brewery, while others thought the brewery's stocks of beer needed protecting from them! Some formed lasting friendships in the village and came back after the war to visit; sadly this battalion suffered particularly heavy casualties and many never returned to England.

Changes on the board

Within a few years of the end of the war the era of Percy Flick's management came to an end. There had already been one bid to take over the firm during the war years, when the Abington Brewery Co in Northampton had made an offer of £40,000 for all the ordinary shares. This had been in 1943 and the offer was rejected, but in 1950 a deal was arranged with members of the Gilchrist family who owned the Burtonwood Brewery in Warrington. Having acquired a controlling share, they took over the management of the company, Percy Flick receiving generous compensation on his retirement in 1951.

6
DELIVERING THE BEER

AT a spectacular Derby Day parade of brewery drays at Epsom race course in 1996, the Hook Norton Brewery team failed to win a prize for its turnout, but instead received a possibly more significant accolade as the only one in the parade which was actually used for delivering beer on a daily basis, rather than being kept simply for promotional and show purposes. The sight of this dray pulled by its well groomed pair of huge shire horses is again a feature of village life in Hook Norton today as it was for a hundred years until shortly after the Second World War.

When John Harris started brewing this was his only means of getting the beer to his customers, not only in the village but much further afield. There can be no doubt that the success of the brewery throughout its history has been partly due to its wide network of customers, first established by John Harris as a largely private trade and later consolidated by his successors concentrating on club and tied house trade, but still extending over a surprisingly wide area for a small family firm. Transport was a key element in this and an interesting analysis carried out in 1913 shows that it cost £2,372 in that year, which represented 10.7 per cent of the total value of all goods delivered to customers. By that date several different forms of transport were in use.

Horses

The advantages for John Harris of running a farm as well as a brewery included not only growing his own barley for malt but also grass, hay and oats to feed the horses which served both operations. After the turn of the century it was clearly not possible to produce all that was needed for the expanded brewery trade and fodder was regularly purchased from other farmers. An order sent by Alban Clarke to Mr Justin Tustian of Milton in 1905 for two or three tons of "old mixture hay" goes on to suggest that "a bit of tasty old sanfoin would suit us well if you have any". No records have survived for the farm but it was clearly an integral part of the business at least until the First World War. The plans for the new brewery stable building in 1894 suggest that eight dray horses were to be accommodated but many more than this appear in the pages of a ledger covering the early years of the twentieth century when John Henry was probably in charge of the stables department.

There were at this time about 30 horses on the books each year, some at the brewery itself, some at the various agencies, but a number were bought and sold during the year. Sales of old horses usually took place at Stow Fair in May, prices ranging from about £15 to £20. There are always some old horses put out to grass and described in the lists as being "in the field", presumably on the farm. Occasionally one died, like "Bob" who died of "heart disease and tumour" on August 11th 1903, or the un-named brown cob who had to be shot in April 1903. Replacements usually came from local farmers, but the prices are not given.

Names like "Captain", "Prince" and "Lion" give an impression of the strength and majesty of these powerful animals who hauled the drays with their heavy loads of full barrels up and down the hilly roads out of Hook Norton. Others have rather less appropriate names – "Dumpling", Jumbo" or "Spot", and several share the same name so that they have to be distinguished by their colour or some

Delivering the Beer

Stable yard at the brewery, c.1910. W. Cross, F. Gardner, W. Beale, C. Austin, J. Pargeter

other feature. In 1902 there were three "Blackbirds", one with a white foot, and one an old horse "in the field", and there were no less than four "Princes" of varying colours. A horse called "Dumpling" appears in the earliest list in 1901 and continued working until 1905 when he was put in the field. Three years later he was described as very lame and was finally "sold to the knacker" in June 1909.

Ten heavy horses were kept at the brewery in 1909, plus two ponies and two cobs, and there were five old horses "in the field". A further thirteen horses, ponies, cobs and a nag were at the stores in Banbury, Shipston, Stratford, Witney and Stow. These would be used for local deliveries or by the outriders when they made their rounds calling on private customers and publicans. Each one had a horse and trap to allow him to cover his area, the cost of which was charged to the brewery. An inventory of 1910 lists 60 sets of harness for different types of vehicle and numerous other items like nosebags, lead reins, halters and collars. This was essential stock which had to be carried and Alban Clarke's rough valuation of it all came to £1,330, a considerable sum in 1910.

A Country Brewery: Hook Norton 1849–1999

A wide variety of vehicles was used, those at the stores being mainly vans, trucks and traps, while at Hook Norton the list included: 7 vans, 5 floats, 8 carts, 3 coal carts, 3 trucks, a trap and a trolley. Some of these would be used for bringing goods to the brewery as well as taking beer out, and the three coal carts would probably make regular journeys to bring coal to the brewery from the railway station at the other end of the village. When they arrived and their loads were tipped in the yard before being shovelled into the boiler house store, women living near the brewery in Scotland End took their washing off the line, or cursed the coal dust that fell on it - a hazard more often associated with the back streets of northern industrial cities than with the rustic charm of a north Oxfordshire village.

Hook Norton is situated in a valley with hills to the north and south which meant steep roads for the horses to climb pulling their heavy loads of full barrels. South Hill on the Chipping Norton road

The dray delivering to The Sun Inn, Hook Norton, 1994. (Photo Mrs G. Hutchinson)

was particularly difficult in the winter when the snow could lie deep on this exposed hilltop. As late as the end of March in 1916 four drays were stranded near Duckpool Farm and men from the brewery had to be sent out to dig a way through the snowdrifts. There were often days in the winter when no drays went out at all because of severe weather, but even in the summer South Hill was so steep that a trace horse had to be added to the team to help pull loaded drays up it. Having reached the top, the extra horse was unhitched, turned around and sent off with a slap on its rump to make its own way back to the brewery. That the horses were capable of finding their way home without help from a driver is born out by the other story told of this (and many other) breweries, which claims that drays could be seen returning to Hook Norton at the end of the day with the drayman sleeping off the effects of his many deliveries to hospitable landlords, while the horses plodded faithfully along the road back to their stables.

The use of horses to deliver the beer was stopped in 1950, but revived again in 1985. Like other breweries, Hook Norton recognised the publicity value of its horse-drawn drays, especially in advertising their traditional style of brewing, and brought one back into service for local deliveries in and around the village. In addition, two other drays have been purchased for appearances at shows and other promotional events. Two shire horses are kept, "Jim" and "Consul", who have been owned by the brewery since about 1994 and whose working lives are likely to be longer than their predecessors at the beginning of the century because they no longer have to pull such heavy loads or undertake such long journeys.

Sending beer by rail

Hook Norton was given its own railway station on the line from Banbury to Cheltenham in 1887, but even before this date the brewery was sending beer to its more distant customers by rail from the station at Chipping Norton. This involved taking the barrels to Chipping Norton by horse and cart first and a further arrangement had to be made at the other end of the journey to deliver them to the customer's door. One of the more distant customers in the 1880s was a Mr A. D. Clarke (possibly a relative) who lived in West Dean near Chichester. On one occasion three kilderkins of ale were dispatched to him by rail from Chipping Norton via Reading and Guildford where they were transferred to the London, Brighton and South Coast Railway and from there to Singleton in Sussex, a few miles from West Dean. An alternative route was tried with the next consignment which was taken by road from the brewery to Chipping Norton, by rail to London where it was transferred to Messrs Pickford & Co's warehouse, eventually completing the journey to Sussex by road in a Pickfords horse-drawn waggon. One wonders what condition the beer was in at the end of this journey. Equally doubtful was the fate of some pale ale sent to a customer in Dry Sandford "left at Oxford to be called for". Even a customer in Charlbury was supplied by rail on several occasions in 1882, a firkin of stout being sent for some reason from the store at Shipston on Stour although it usually went from Chipping Norton. Occasionally other goods were sent, and at Christmas 1882 John Harris sent personal gifts of a turkey each to a Mrs Preston in Brackley and Mrs Chivers in Bradford on Avon – long before the days of refrigerated vans. The real value of the railway, however, was in supplying distant customers, enabling the brewery to extend its market far beyond the reach of drayhorses. There were a number of London customers at different times, and the regular trade established in Cheltenham and around Quenington (probably using family contacts in Gloucestershire) was dependent on the railways.

Sometimes there were problems, and letters had to be written to Mr Beechey the Station Master employed by the Great Western Railway at Hook Norton. In November 1899 and again a year later the time taken to deliver consignments of ale to Cheltenham was a particular concern: "Our customers complain very much of not receiving their goods till late on Friday or Saturday night, the goods having been started from here on Wednesday. Unless a better delivery can be made we shall lose our trade in Cheltenham." Then there were problems with rough handling of empty casks. In February 1900 the brewery claimed compensation for an 18 gallon cask received from Birmingham "in a smashed condition – all the staves on one side were completely crushed and broken as though some heavy trucks had passed over it." Even more suspicious was the disappearance of a full 5 gallon cask of ale from a truck load sent from Hook Norton station to Fairford. "It appears to have been lost in transit."

The steam wagon

The most exciting development in the brewery's transport arrangements in the early twentieth century was the purchase of a steam powered wagon for use on the road in 1904. Other breweries were investing in such vehicles and Alban Clarke was not going to be left behind either in making savings on the cost of transport or in showing that Hook Norton was keeping up with the latest technology. He showed proper caution, however, and wrote first to Mr Kench of Edmunds & Kench Ltd of Banbury for information about the wagon they had already purchased. The reply was reassuring, Mr Kench reckoning that "it does the work of six horses, and if we could keep it going within a radius of 7 or 8 miles it would do the work of ten." He thought it would be best for moving large loads from Hook Norton to Banbury, rather than "your two horse journeys where you drop casks here and there".

Alban was persuaded, and an order was sent off to Mann & Co of Hunslett near Leeds. Founded in 1897 as Mann & Charlesworth, they had become Mann & Co in 1900 and were making a name for themselves in this field. They had just patented (with Claytons) a new design of wagon with a crossflow boiler which had the boiler placed sideways across the front of the vehicle, reducing the danger of boiling dry when the normal type of boiler was tipped by going up steep hills. Although this might have been appropriate to Hook Norton, the wagon chosen was of the conventional type, and Alban was anxious to have it delivered as soon as possible.

He was also aware of its value in advertising the firm and his initial order was followed the next day by another letter setting out the colour scheme to be used, "the engine and wagon to be painted a dark chocolate picked out with red". There were to be name boards on both sides of the wagon, and "we hope you will make the engine and body of the wagon as smart as possible as well as the advertise-

The Steam Wagon. First supplied by Mann's of Leeds in 1904, it remained in use until about 1910

ment boards. It will then provide us with an excellent advertisement on the roads". He also specified removable rails on both sides for retaining the barrels. However, he was somewhat less concerned about the comfort of the driver, having "upon consideration" decided to save money and dispense with the driver's shelter.

As for training the driver, that was a matter of some importance as no-one at Hook Norton had experience of anything other than horses. Alban requested that initial training should be provided by Mann's at their works in Leeds. "We will probably choose an intelligent young man who has been employed here some eight years, and who is very anxious to become thoroughly proficient." Mann's agreed, but when John Bloxham the "intelligent young man" selected by Clarke arrived in Leeds they were apparently not very impressed with him. Perhaps the Yorkshiremen, engineers in a big city, saw him as a slow-witted country yokel from the rural south. The manager wrote to say that they found poor Bloxham rather slow and were not sure that he was up to the task. Alban's reply, while supporting Bloxham and pointing out that he was especially keen to take up this work because his two brothers were both drivers of steam wagons, concludes by saying "it is quite possible he may appear a bit slow in learning, but the lad has good solid qualities which will overcome difficulties". It is perhaps significant that when the new wagon was delivered in May it was arranged that the driver from Leeds should stay at Hook Norton for a fortnight to give Bloxham "a good start in the driving", and ten days later Alban asked Mann's "will there be any inconvenience if we engage him for the next four weeks at least?" Young Bloxham's name does not appear in the wages book and in subsequent years the wagon was invariably driven by John Hall, one of the draymen, who received 1s per day extra wages for it.

Alban was proud of the new wagon and had it photographed with a full load. He also had it included in the foreground of the painting of the new brewery on the advertising poster which had just been commissioned, where it still appears today. At the end of the first year he did a cost analysis which showed that the wagon, costing £525, would pay for itself by reducing transport costs within the first three years. The savings included "six horses @ 12s. per week, labour £75 (presumably in the stables), and reduction of the railway account £150". These and other savings amounted to £442, while the running costs came to £230, the largest items being £73 wages, £71 for fuel – probably coke, and nearly £22 for oil and grease. A stock of spare parts worth £20 was carried at the brewery because repairs would obviously have to be carried out locally, though on one occasion a mechanic from Mann's came down to deal with a persistent problem. In general, however, the steam wagon seems to have given good service for about six years. In 1909 it suffered a major breakdown when the piston rod and the cylinder cover broke "some twenty miles from home". In a subsequent letter to Mann's it is described as "an old type of engine". In 1910 the wages item disappears from the accounts suggesting that the wagon stopped being used at about that time.

Not everyone was happy with the new type of vehicle, however; in particular Mr G. F. Braggins a Banbury timber merchant and ornamental oak gate manufacturer ("under royal patronage" according to his letterhead – and therefore a man to be taken seriously), who had an unfortunate encounter with this clanking and hissing monster while driving in his horse-drawn phaeton. He wrote to complain angrily that "the loaded wagon and the smoke and noise of gearing was enough to frighten anything". His mare shied, jumped onto the pathway and he nearly lost control – "Had there been a woman driving the phaeton, a very serious accident might have occurred".

Equally upset was Mr Howse the Ramsden blacksmith, a man used to horses rather than mechanical giants. On a summer day in 1904 he was peacefully riding his bicycle in the narrow lanes around the village when he suddenly encountered the brewery steam wagon filling the roadway and coming steadily towards him: "I met it in a very narrow part of the road . . . he kept coming on at the same speed and I had to throw myself off the cycle into the hedge to save being run over which is not a very pleasant experience". One can only agree with him. This incident occurred during the first few weeks of the wagon's use and it may have been that the driver (was it the unfortunate Bloxham on a training run?) was inexperienced. In any case such a vehicle would not have been easy to control or to manoeuvre quickly on narrow roads, the steering mechanism being operated by the driver rapidly turning a wheel which moved the front axle, and then turning it in the opposite direction to straighten up again.

To both complaints Alban Clarke replied briefly that he would see the men when they returned and "hear what they had to say about it". One gets the impression that he would be likely to defend his new toy. He was much more sympathetic when writing to a local farmer about an incident involving one of the horse drays (showing that it was not only the new technology which could cause surprising accidents): "We beg to acknowledge receipt of yours of the 13th, and very much regret to hear that one of our draymen ran over one of your sheep. We should very much like to bring the culprit to book."

Personal transport

One or two scraps of evidence illustrate the way the Managing Director and other staff travelled. The most frequent travellers were the outriders who generally used a horse and trap. When agents or other contractors were called to a meeting at the Brewery they sometimes found it convenient to come by train, as did Mr Toy coming from Chipping Norton, and meetings were sometimes fixed to fit in with the arrival time of trains. When they had to look over a public house the brewery was thinking of buying in Chipping Warden near Banbury, Alban Clarke sent a telegram to Toy asking him what train he was likely to travel on so that he could also join it at Hook Norton. "I will arrange for a covered conveyance to meet us at Banbury station and drive straight to Chipping Warden."

The Managing Director's motor in about 1910. The man standing at the side usually acted as chauffeur but for the photograph Alban Clarke preferred to be at the wheel himself

Alban was a keen cyclist and apparently used his cycle for business as well as pleasure, even planning to cycle as far as Statford on Avon on one occasion. He wrote to the tenant of The Swan in Stratford whom he had arranged to visit "If the weather is unsuitable for cycling I shall come by the usual train on Wednesday". Stratford is about 20 miles from Hook Norton. One of the outrides at the time of the First War was receiving £5 a month allowance for a bicycle, suggesting that he used this means of travel instead of the usual horse and trap.

A little earlier there is mention in the wages book of ½d. a mile being paid to the driver of a motor car, perhaps for the use of the managing director, and certainly in Percy Flick's time he persuaded the directors to meet half the cost of a new motor car – "not to exceed £100" – and all the petrol costs for business journeys, the justification being that it was felt important to maintain the company's goodwill by regular contact with customers, especially in the Coventry club trade. He is remembered as being driven by a chauffeur.

Motor lorries

In 1927 the directors do not seem to have greeted the idea of using motor transport for the first time with any great eagerness. Their first recorded discussion of it refers to the "possibility of the Company being forced to adopt motor traction owing to the state of the roads", as if it was something they were only considering with great reluctance. As far as Percy Flick was concerned this was probably true, as he saw the purchase of a lorry as an unnecessary expense. The problem suggested by the reference to "the state of the roads", was that by the late 1920s many of the rough stone roads in the countryside had been treated with tarmac providing a hardwearing smooth surface suitable for the rubber tyres of motor vehicles, but quite unsuited to horses' hooves which slipped dangerously on it, especially when hauling heavy loads up and down hills. Whether this was the deciding factor or simply the wish to keep up with developments in other breweries and perhaps adopt a more cost-effective form of transport, the decision was taken to buy the brewery's first motor lorry at the end of 1928. It was a 30cwt. Morris from the County Garages in Banbury and cost £331 13s. 4d., plus a further £25 for the road fund licence.

This lorry lasted for about four years and was traded in for £60 against a new Bedford purchased from Ewins Garage for £250 in 1933. This in turn was replaced at the beginning of 1937 by another Bedford which probably remained in use throughout the war, when purchase of new vehicles for non-essential purposes would have been restricted. There were also severe restrictions on the use of petrol during the war and by 1944 under the Motor Fuel Rationing Regulations it was necessary to make applications for fuel a month at a time. There was also the possibility of vehicles and their drivers being requisitioned in an emergency, and the brewery, like other businesses, received a circular requesting it to make sure that vehicles were kept in good order and ready for instant use. A note at the foot of the petrol application form stresses the need to "take care of your tyres and be sure to submit them for replacement when they are smooth." In such circumstances the horses, which had remained in use alongside the lorries, kept local deliveries going throughout the war years and for some time afterwards.

Lorries began to take over all of the delivery work and horses were phased out in the early 1950s, when first Bedford and later Albion "Chieftain" and "Claymore" vehicles with specially built bodywork were in use. For some years an additional lorry and driver from Chipping Norton was hired for one or two days a week to do the Coventry run and to help with other deliveries. As trade has expanded since the 1970s the number of vehicles has been increased to cope with the greater volume of deliveries and the wider area to be covered. In 1999 the fleet consists of five lorries and two vans delivering over a radius of approximately 80 miles around Hook Norton. This includes bulk deliveries to the depots of distribution companies who carry Hook Norton beer to a much wider area. In addition there is once again a horse-drawn dray delivering to pubs in and around the village, reviving the tradition of 150 years.

7

BILL CLARKE

The revival of real ale

AT the time of his father's accident in 1917 Bill Clarke was only thirteen and still at school in Burford. Clearly it would be some years before he could take his place in the family firm and it was fortunate that Percy Flick had already taken over from Alban Clarke as Managing Director. Even when her son was old enough Flick advised Frances Clarke against letting Bill join the firm, suggesting that the poor state of trade in the early 1920s and the brewery's uncertain future would not guarantee him a living. So for a few years he worked on a farm in Gloucestershire, farming having always been the family's second interest. In 1928, however, he came back to Hook Norton and entered the brewery. There is little indication that the economic state of the business was any better than it had been a few years earlier, so perhaps it was family pressure or Bill's own determination that persuaded Flick to find room for him at that time. He worked at first as Assistant under the head brewer Frank Beale, who had been there since the 1890s. In 1934 he became a director and took his place on the board. Flick had found him work in the office when old Mr Stratford died, but urged the

William Clarke, 1904–1982

directors to consider the extension and modernisation of the bottling plant "to give more scope for the employment of Mr Clarke and to give him a better chance of progressing in the business". Bill Clarke was to spend the next 50 years "progressing in the business", acquiring an unrivalled practical knowledge of brewing and of the day to day running of the operation.

The Gilchrist connection

All but a few of the 2500 ordinary shares in the Hook Norton Brewery Company Ltd were owned by the Clarke family until 1951 when Bill's sisters Nancy and Frances Mary decided to sell their holding in order to make use of their capital in other ways, thus creating something of a crisis. Bill was not in a position to purchase their shares and they may have been unwilling to offer them to Percy Flick even if he wished to buy them. There was undoubtedly some tension between him and the two sisters and in any case he was by now 74 and probably thinking of retiring. In these circumstances a new backer had to be found to invest in the company and the Gilchrist family, who owned the much larger but also independent Burtonwood Brewery at Warrington, were ideal candidates. The result of the negotiation was that they purchased not only the shares belonging to the two sisters, but also most of Bill's as well, so that they ended up with a large majority holding in the company. Percy Flick retired and the Gilchrists took the three vacant seats on the board with Mrs Mary Gilchrist as Managing Director and Chairman, Ian as Assistant MD and Norman as the third member. Bill Clarke continued as a director and was appointed Managing Brewer.

This team proved an ideal partnership, the Gilchrists bringing their experience of managing a larger concern while leaving Bill in charge of the day to day running of the brewery at a local level – the level he knew so well and was so good at. There is little evidence of tension between the two families on the board, rather the relationship seems to have developed into one of mutual trust and respect for each other's expertise.

Some important decisions were taken almost immediately. It had already been suggested that the bottling operation at the brewery should be expanded and once the Gilchrists had inspected the site they authorised the purchase of new bottling machinery and the conversion of the old malthouse for this purpose. At the same time Bill Clarke suggested the introduction of a new bitter beer (which was also bottled under the name "Jackpot") and this was agreed. This was the first bitter brewed at Hook Norton for some time, only mild having been produced throughout the war years. Four months later sales of bitter were exceeding expectations. A practical advantage of the Gilchrist connection was felt immediately when new machinery for bottling or new supplies of casks, bottles and cases were being purchased, since at Burtonwood they already had wider contacts in the trade and were used to buying much larger quantities than Hook Norton. It was invariably Ian Gilchrist who made enquiries and obtained the best price for anything major that was required at Hook Norton.

Rather less successful was the initiative taken by the new Managing Director. Mary Gilchrist brought a woman's eye to the question of the brewery's image as projected by the appearance of the public houses it owned. She reported to one of the first meetings of the new directors that she did not approve of the colour schemes being used, and proposed that all the tied houses should be painted in a uniform style. Her suggested colours were contrasting combinations of either blue and primrose or black and yellow. At a subsequent meeting Bill reported back that "no decorator would recommend blue for exterior work" and so she had to settle for black and yellow. When the first two pubs had been painted the directors went to view them and Mrs. Gilchrist declared herself well pleased. It was agreed to paint all the others in similar style. However, the brightness of the black and yellow on old buildings in a village street alarmed some of the locals and horrified the planning officers who had been appointed under the recent Town and Country Planning Act. The following year the board had to agree to tone down the colour scheme of the Company's houses to meet the requirements of the Act, and in 1955 there was a lot of criticism from local residents in Brailes when their pub was repainted, and the directors agreed to vary the colour scheme when used on old stone houses.

While such bright colours might look all right in the urban environment of Warrington, they were clearly less appropriate in rural Oxfordshire, but what is significant about this episode is perhaps not the actual colours chosen so much as the concept of a house style. The Gilchrists knew the value of promoting a corporate image and were ahead of others in the industry by making

Burtonwood one of the first breweries to advertise in the new media of television.

Upgrading the tied estate

During the 1950s and 1960s government legislation put breweries all over the country under new pressure to upgrade the facilities in their tied houses and Hook Norton found itself in receipt of complaints from local authority Sanitary Inspectors as well as Planning Officers. This was not just a matter of changing the colour of the paint on the outside of the building, but rather more costly improvements to the toilets – or in some cases the provision of proper toilets for the first time. There were still rural pubs where no flush toilets of any sort existed, as indeed there were many cottages without such facilities. A bucket in a shed at the bottom of the garden was still all that many village people enjoyed at home, and provision in some pubs amounted to even less, with no provision at all for women, who were not specially catered for in such pubs either in the design and decoration of bar accommodation or elsewhere. Sanitary Inspectors required the provision of separate facilities for "Gents" and "Ladies" up to modern standards of hygiene. This was expensive for the brewery, significantly increasing costs and reducing profits at a time when sales were not high. In September 1956 when the Company experienced a "sharp drop" in trade the Sanitary Authority was demanding improvements to several public houses. Such demands continued in subsequent years, and although sales and profits increased, building work at the pubs was always a drain on resources. In 1961 the directors arranged to meet the Surveyor from the Banbury Rural District Council to discuss the work being demanded on the pubs at Epwell and Wigginton and to explain the problem of having to spend large sums of money on small country houses where the profits did not seem to justify the expense, but to the local authority it was simply a matter of public hygiene and not related to profits. At least three other pubs, The Albion Tavern Chipping Norton, the New Inn Abthorpe and The Coach and Horses in Banbury, were all listed for improvements by three different councils at the same time as the ones in Epwell and Wigginton. If such work was not carried out there was always the danger that the licence would not be renewed at the next brewster sessions in the magistrates court.

Equally worrying was the possibility that the brewery would not be able to attract tenants for its houses, and demands for improvement of the living accommodation often came from this quarter as standards of living and the expectations of prospective tenants rose. There was also the need to make bar areas brighter and more welcoming in order to attract new customers, including women in the "swinging sixties", and to provide car parking and food as well as drink in the larger houses. The final irony was that once such improvements had been carried out, the pub became liable for higher rates to the local authority. Although expensive at the time, however, such upgrading represented an investment and the tied estate remained an enormously valuable asset to the Company.

One of the attractions which some customers were coming to expect in the bar was a "fruit machine", but in 1963 the directors, while aware that some breweries were installing them, refused permission to Hook Norton tenants "as there was some doubt about their legality". Two years later they discussed the matter again at length and finally agreed to allow them on a cost sharing basis between the tenant, the supplier and the brewery. Even then they were of the opinion that the takings would not justify installing them in the smaller country pubs.

After all this expenditure on improvements of one sort or another it was essential to maximize the returns and publicity was very important. Special re-opening ceremonies were arranged which were reported by the local press, with photographs of the new facilities. When work was completed on The Coach and Horses in Banbury it was opened by the Mayor and it was reported to the directors a few months later that trade had increased considerably. The Rose and Crown in Chipping Warden was opened in 1969 by Mr Richard Courage, current President of the Licensed Victuallers Association.

The club trade in the post-war years

Trade with working men's clubs in the Coventry and Rugby areas continued to be the mainstay of the Company's sales in the period after the Second World War just as it had been before. It was particularly valuable in compensating for any decline in public house trade during these years due to the growth of rival entertainments and the attractions of home drinking. Indeed the clubs themselves, with their lower prices and programmes of entertainment and sport for their members, drew customers away from the pubs, but Hook Norton had a share in both markets. There were at least twelve clubs in Coventry on the Company's books in the 1950s including old customers like the Vauxhall Club, Binley Colliery Club and Coventry Engineers. In Rugby there were the Railwaymen's and the Engineers, while closer to home the Company supplied British Legion Clubs in Chipping Norton, Deddington and Moreton in Marsh. There was no political bias as Hook Norton beer was sold equally in Banbury Conservative Club and the Northampton Trades and Labour Club. In many cases the link with these clubs was cemented by loans from the brewery to finance enlargements and improvements to their facilities. These were usually conditional on a trading agreement to sell only Hook Norton draught beer and the amount of interest was geared to the number of barrels consumed. The deal suited both sides, and the brewery was prepared to lend quite substantial sums to a large club in Willenhall which was already selling eighteen or nineteen barrels a week in 1958 and would expect to sell more when its premises were enlarged. In the early 1960s the club trade had grown so much that Bill Clarke could no longer manage it himself and a Traveller was appointed to look after the Coventry and Rugby areas, leaving Bill free to concentrate on the rest of his duties.

Village activities

Some of Bill Clarke's other duties were concerned with activities outside the brewery. Like his father, he was involved with many

Retirement party for Harold Wyton in 1969 after 60 years with the firm. Left to right: J. Stratford, P. Heritage, C. Hazard, A. Cadd, P. Hemmings, D. Clarke, Bill Clarke, R. Atkinson, W. Wells

aspects of life in Hook Norton and was a well known figure at every village event. He continued the family tradition of supporting the volunteer Fire Brigade, joining it in 1928, the year he came back to Hook Norton and went into the brewery. He became its Chief Officer and continued to serve until 1959. It is said that the only time he failed to turn out in answer to the siren was when it went off during his daughter's wedding in the parish church. On that occasion the Chief Officer was missing when the engine rushed off to deal with a fire at Sibford. His support of the Brigade included encouraging other brewery employees to become volunteer firemen, and allowing them to drop their work and leave the brewery immediately the call came. This was particularly frequent during the war when the Hook Norton engine might be called on to support others much farther away than its normal area of operation, once going as far as Southampton. Such calls meant long absences from work and the brewery had to function without some of its workforce.

He was also a member of the Parish Council for over 30 years and served as its Vice-Chairman, helping to run the village with the same benevolent concern that he showed when managing the brewery. On Sundays he was to be seen at St Peter's parish church with the family, where he became a sidesman and later, almost inevitably, Churchwarden. In addition he served as Treasurer of the village Horticultural Society and the Hook Norton Band, helping and promoting their interests in every way.

Bill Clarke's role in local life meant that he knew most families in the village personally and when particular skills were needed at the brewery he could go straight to the right person and recruit them, knowing their background and their working reputation. At the beginning of 1960 the brewery office was short staffed, so he went to see John Stratford who was then working at Alcan, the Banbury aluminium company, where he had been since the war. No doubt Bill knew he had the skills that were needed, but he would also have known that John Stratford was the grandson of the Mr Stratford who had been an outride for the brewery in the early part of the century. He simply asked him to come and "help with the books" to which he agreed, and stayed to become Company Secretary and a director, eventually retiring in 1991. In equally casual style he later persuaded him to help out as Parish Clerk when a new one was needed, "just to try it for a year" – he stayed for 25. On another occasion he stopped to talk to a builder at work in the village, Fred Gardner whose family also had long associations with the brewery, and offered him work repairing and maintaining brewery property which became permanent employment. There was no difficulty in persuading men to come and work there because of the affection people felt for the brewery and for Bill Clarke personally.

The crisis for draught beer

Beer was being brewed at Hook Norton at this time both for sale as draught and for bottling. The draught beer in wooden casks was traditionally the main product on which the reputation and the profits of the brewery had always been based but in the late 1960s changes were taking place at a national level which altered the balance in favour of bottled beers. Hook Norton's main output was still mild, the traditional drink of the south Midlands, but this too was being threatened by a growing preference for bitter. The total sales of draught beer in 1955 amounted to 5,456 barrels which nearly doubled to 10,141 by 1965, but then began to decline steadily. The directors noted with increasing dismay a drop of about 400 barrels in each of the next two years, about 75 per cent of which was in sales of mild. Even in the Coventry clubs draught beers, and especially mild were losing favour. The news was not completely bad because the brewery had invested in new bottling plant and increased its output in this area where demand was still rising. But it required the purchase of further equipment to cope with the greater volume of bottling, and although turnover increased, profits remained static or declined slightly for a time.

The crisis for traditional breweries like Hook Norton, which was at its worst in the late 1960s and early '70s, derived from the marketing by the big nationals of bottled lager and of mass-produced beers distributed in pressurised "kegs". They were able to benefit from economies of scale and rapid production methods which reduced labour and energy costs, and were successful in creating a demand for their products which were very different from those produced by the small breweries using traditional methods. The situation seemed so bad that the directors even considered retailing a keg beer under the Hook Norton name in 1967 but "resolved not to proceed with it at the present time". Two years later they entered a trading agreement with Whitbread Flowers to sell "Tankard" and "Gold Label" in about a dozen Hook Norton houses, and Heineken Lager "where there was any demand for it". In return they leased four local Whitbread houses for 21 years at a peppercorn rent. These were The Wellington at Moreton in Marsh, The Churchill at Paxford, The Gate Inn at Brailes and The New Inn at Whichford (which had once been part of their own estate). Because of intense competition from other brands they were forced to offer a bonus on sales of Hook Norton bottled beers in the clubs.

CAMRA and the revival of real ale

By 1973 sales of Hook Norton draught had fallen to 6942 barrels, the lowest figure for fifteen years, but a remarkable change was about to happen. Two years earlier the Campaign For Real Ale had been launched with the aim of reviving interest in traditionally brewed, full flavoured beer as opposed to the rather gassy, homogeneous keg beers which seemed to be taking over the whole market. Expertly organised, the Campaign became one of the most effective consumer movements of the period and succeeded in checking the trend towards mass produced beer just in time to save the special character of small independent breweries like Hook Norton from extinction. The sales figures speak for themselves: having sunk to under 7,000 barrels in 1973 they began to rise, slowly at first and then more rapidly, reaching 15,000 by 1978 and over 20,000 in the early 1980s. The Chairman expressed his pleasure at the increased turnover in these years, but particularly because it was due to increased sales of Hook Norton's own beer rather than distribution of other brands.

The effect of CAMRA was not only to boost sales of draught beer, but also to create interest in the traditional brewing process and requests began to come in for permission to visit the brewery. In May and June 1977 two open weekends were held when visitors flocked to see the remarkable tower brewery and its steam powered machinery still operating much as in Alban Clarke's time. One element of the plant he had installed was no longer able to cope, however, and the Thames Water Authority demanded a new waste filtering system to replace the existing one which had been working for 70 years. The cost was reduced by using the brewery labour force to assist the contractors, a practice of which Alban would have approved.

An extra fermenting vessel had to be added in order to cope with the increased output and two widely differing quotes were received, so that Mr Gilchrist was asked to make enquiries at Burtonwood to see what was thought reasonable and to see if anything was known about the firms in question. It was another example of Hook Norton benefiting from the wider experience available at Burtonwood.

The business relationship between the Gilchrist and Clarke families continued to flourish and in 1974 Bill Clarke was appointed Managing Director with the full confidence of the Gilchrists who were increasingly happy to leave the running of the business in his hands. Meanwhile his son David, having served his pupillage at Burtonwood before returning to Hook Norton, moved into the position of Head Brewer.

Bill Clarke retired in 1981 after more than 50 years with the firm during which he had witnessed huge changes in the wider world outside Hook Norton, changes which included a major shift in public tastes for beer. He died early the following year, much lamented in brewery and village. People still alive today who remember him invariably say what a nice man he was, recalling that in spite of his senior position he was always approachable and could often be found in the bar of The Sun or The Pear Tree; "He'd always talk to you and buy you a drink" is one of their most frequent comments. When at the next meeting of the board the remaining directors paid tribute to him as a person and to his work for the brewery, the Chairman suggested that "instead of standing in silence, we should raise our glasses to him".

8
THE BREWING PROCESS

ON dark winter mornings or bright summer ones, work starts in the brewery at 6.0 a.m. when the steam engine is started up, and its rythmic thumping and hissing provides the background to everything else that happens in the brewery throughout the day.

Mashing

The clear fresh water from underground wells has been pumped up to the cold liquor tank high up under the roof of the tower brewery, where there are wonderful views over the waking village and the fields beyond. Some of this liquor is drawn off to be boiled ready for use in the day's brewing. Sacks of Maris Otter malt, used because it imparts a good malty flavour even in a fairly low strength beer, have been screened and crushed in the grist mill and are now released into the Steele's Patent Masher where the grains are thoroughly mixed with hot liquor, ensuring that every single one is soaked before being run into the mash tun. Revolving rakes slowly stir the mixture for a short time and then the mash is left to stand for two

A Country Brewery: Hook Norton 1849–1999

Mash tun

Filling the copper

hours, while the natural enzymes in the malt convert its starch into sugars. At the end of this process the resulting liquid, now called wort, is slowly run off into the copper while more hot liquor is sprayed over the grains held back in the bottom of the mash tun to extract all remaining sugars in a process called "sparging". (The spent grains are collected daily by local farmers for cattle feed, just as the hops are recycled as a fertilizer, so nothing is wasted.)

Boiling and adding hops

By about 11 o'clock the mashing and sparging is all done and the huge copper is full of wort. Now the hops are added and the whole brew is boiled for an hour and twenty minutes. Clouds of steam find their way out through the vents of the copper house roof and the air is filled with the aroma of hops and malt which greets visitors fortunate enough to arrive at this time. (If they care to look up at the century-old copper house roof they will see that the slates are laid in such a way that the steam can escape between them). Boiling sterilises the wort and dissolves oils in the hops which give the beer its subtle bitter flavour as well as improving its keeping qualities. Three different varieties – Fuggles, Golding and Challenger – are blended to give the distinctive Hook Norton taste.

After boiling, the contents of the copper are transferred to the hopback – a vessel which lives up to its simple name by acting as a sieve and keeping the hops back when the wort is strained through perforated plates on its floor. There is more to it than this, however, because the hop flowers themselves get matted together in a layer above these plates and themselves help to filter out unwanted protein which would otherwise result in hazy beer. From the hopback the wort is pumped all the way up to the top floor for cooling.

Cooling

Under the louvres of the roof at the top of this part of the building is a wide, shallow open cooler where the near-boiling wort begins to cool down ready for fermentation. This open cooler is one of the last of its kind still being used but it is now supplemented by a modern paraflow cooler into which the wort runs next. The temperature is brought down to 62°F before gravity takes the wort down to the next level for the fermenting stage.

Fermentation

It is now about 3.30 in the afternoon and the huge fermenting vessel to be used for this brew is filling up. Here some more sterile liquor is added to adjust the brew to the desired strength (its original gravity). Then the yeast is added and stirred in to make sure that it permeates the whole brew. The process of fermentation consists of the yeast converting sugars in the wort to alcohol. It takes seven days to achieve the desired level, and during this time the brew remains in the fermenting room alongside other vessels full of fermenting wort at various stages of the process. The delicious aroma of malt and hops elsewhere in the brewery is mixed here with a less pleasant atmosphere of carbon dioxide given off during the process. At regular intervals the temperature is checked and has to be carefully controlled. Some of the yeast, which is continually growing and threatening to overflow the high sides of the vessel, is removed down a conical chute to be cooled and stored for use in future brewings.

After five days some yeast still remains suspended in the brew and the temperature is lowered to 58°F, causing most of this to settle to the bottom, although it is important that some remains to give the beer a protective covering in the fermenting vessel and for conditioning in the cask. The brewer's aim is a consistent level of residual yeast in every brew.

Racking and dry hopping

From the fermentation room the beer is run off into tanks on the ground floor where it is allowed to settle for several hours before being put into casks. It is at this stage that one of the most traditional practices is carried out, that of adding a handful of best quality dry hops to each cask as it is filled. Few breweries take the trouble to do

The Brewing Process

Wort passing through the open cooler

Fermentation in progress

this today, but at Hook Norton it is looked upon as an essential feature in giving their beer its special quality and they intend to continue the practice just as it has been done since John Harris's day.

Finally the casks are sent down to the cellar where finings are added before the beer eventually leaves the brewery. A week or two later it will fill someone's glass, perhaps at The Pear Tree almost next to the brewery, or in a pub a hundred miles away.

9

DAVID AND JAMES CLARKE

~

The brewery today and tomorrow

L IKE most of the Clarke family children, David's earliest memories of the brewery are of playing in and around the buildings from an early age. At junior school in Banbury he normally travelled there and back by bus, but once a week his great treat was to be brought home by the brewery lorry returning from the weekly Coventry run. He grew up with the brewery as part of his life. In 1959 he began formally to learn the trade at first hand, following the traditional practice of going to another brewery to work as a pupil – appropriately in his case at the Gilchrist's Burtonwood brewery near Warrington.

Developments in bottling

After a pupillage of fifteen months David returned in April 1960 to work under his father's guidance at Hook Norton, particularly in the bottling plant, the area where Bill had himself started more than 30 years earlier. It was by now a rather different and more important part of the operation than it had been. The output of bottled beers

David Clarke, 1941–

had increased steadily even in the 1950s and 1960s when draught was in decline, and it continued to grow. One of the Gilchrist's first actions at Hook Norton had been to expand bottling, setting up new plant in the former malthouse, and as output grew so additional machinery had to be purchased to cope with the demand. This was often reconditioned equipment for reasons of economy but it was a great advance on the hand methods originally employed to fill each bottle from the casks. A powered crown cork machine was installed in 1965 after Mr Gilchrist had "made enquiries in the north" in order to get the best price. Previously screwtop bottles were used which were individually sealed by hand. Later improvements included new equipment for pasteurising and filtering the beer as well as labelling the bottles.

Hook Norton brewed bitter for bottling under their own Jackpot label as well as a brown ale, but for many years it also undertook the bottling of Guinness under licence. This was a trade which had begun before the First World War. Originally the beer was brought to Hook Norton in hogsheads, but in more recent times it was obviously more efficient to use road tankers, and further savings were made for the Guinness company by shipping larger and larger quantities. Wishing to keep the contract, Hook Norton had to enlarge its storage capacity, purchasing a new tank for this purpose, but eventually the cost of keeping up with the reqirements of this contract outweighed the advantages. To continue would have meant renewing much of the bottling plant, which was beginning to wear out, and in addition new machinery was needed to handle the gold foil cap now added to the Guinness bottle. The decision was taken to discontinue bottling both Guinness and their own beers at Hook Norton in 1986.

New arrangements have been made since then for the bottling of Hook Norton beers by other breweries with the necessary plant to deal with this aspect of the market. A new type of outlet – the large supermarket chain – has also developed, and some now stock Old Hooky in particular regions while Tesco sells it nationwide. "Green" unconditioned beer is sent from Hook Norton to be conditioned, bottled and distributed from other centres. It is a convenient arrangement which allows Hook Norton to concentrate on what they feel they do best – brewing the beer.

Continuity and change

David Clarke succeeded his father as Managing Director in 1981 and continues to run the brewery in the '90s, having been joined in turn by his son James, now Head Brewer. Thus the family tradition continues. Some things change, however, and one of the most noticeable breaks with tradition is the presence of David's wife Paula on the staff. Earlier wives and daughters of the family have played a part as directors and shareholders, but seem to have been kept at a distance from the brewery itself. Doris Cadd, a long serving retired employee, remembers as a child peeping through the hedge at

"Brooklyn", then the Clarke residence, and admiring the very lady-like figures of Frances Elizabeth Clarke and her sister walking in the garden years ago. Such enforced leisure and segregation of wives from their husband's business are no longer acceptable and Paula Clarke is to be seen around the office every day, busily tapping away at her computer keyboard, answering telephones and helping to organise the Managing Director's schedule in her capacity as his personal secretary. She also helps with the administration of the tied trade. She is almost certainly the first female member of the family to be so directly involved in the business.

There is more to be done in the brewery than brewing beer. Every morning there is a busy routine of telephoning tenants and other customers for their orders to be delivered in two day's time. These are then processed by computer to produce cellar sheets and draymen's tickets. Later on in the cellar and bottle store the loads are made up for the next day. The casks and cases are prepared, together with wines and spirits and other brands of beer being distributed and draymen load and unload in the yard. Meanwhile the continuous routine of administering the company's financial affairs is handled by the Company Secretary, and the Reps are in and out visiting customers while in the main office downstairs the Receptionist expertly handles everything from incoming telephone calls, deliveries and casual visitors wanting to see the steam engine or buy some beer, while hopefully finding time to get on with her other work. As befits a small family firm management styles are as traditional as the beer, staff are identified by their own first names rather than by job titles, relationships are personal and both David and James Clarke lead their team like members of a large family. When a member of that team died recently the whole brewery closed and the horsedrawn dray turned out for the funeral, with the Managing Director and other staff walking behind it.

About 36 people are currently employed, most of whom live in Hook Norton. Some of these are the second or third generation of their families to work there, and there are husbands and wives or fathers and sons working together. The brewery benefits from this local reserve of skills as the village does from the availability of employment opportunities close to home, helping to keep the

The Hook Norton football team sponsored by the brewery

village alive and flourishing as a community at a time when others are becoming mere dormitories for commuters.

The family's involvement with the life of the village has not declined. Their traditional connection with the volunteer Fire Brigade is as strong as ever. David was its Chief Officer for many years, being awarded the BEM in recognition of his contribution, undoubtedly the most important part of which was to lead the successful campaign in 1981 to preserve the village's own retained unit. If James ever considered an alternative to going into the brewery it would have been to make a full-time career in the fire service. He has succeeded in combining this interest with the family brewery just as previous generations have done and is now the local brigade's Chief Officer, perhaps one of the youngest in the service to hold that position. The brewery's support is also important to the success of the Hook Norton band and the village football team, both directly sponsored by the brewery, and David has been both bellringer and sidesman at St Peter's church. In the most recent development at the brewery the Hook Norton Local History Society is to be given space in the new Visitor Centre to store its

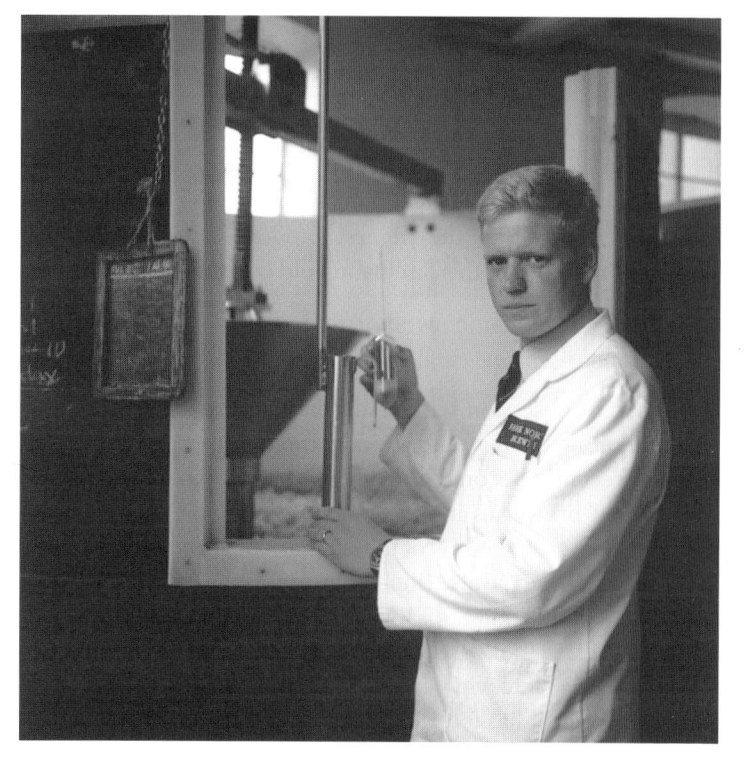

James Clarke, Head Brewer and fifth generation of the founding family

the edge of Hook Norton saw much less trade after the railway from which it took its name was closed in the 1960s, although it was not sold off until some years later. A major improvement took place in the very centre of the village in 1991 when the Red Lion and The Sun Inn, two rival establishments which stood next door to each other, were made into a single pub offering improved facilities. The Fox Hotel in the market place at Chipping Norton was purchased from Hall's Oxford Brewery and several others from Whitbreads, including some of those formerly leased under a trading agrement. The Trumpet at Evesham brought the number of Hook Norton houses up to 39 in 1999.

Hook Norton beer is available much more widely in the 1990s than in earlier periods through the distribution companies and supermarket chains. A strong brand image is important in this kind of market and Old Hooky in particular has been successful in achieving this, although the company would not wish to become dependent on a single product. In recent years it has won several important awards which help to maintain its reputation. Having won the silver medal in the Brewing Industry International Awards in 1996 for their best bitter, two years later the same beer was Champion Cask Ale while Old Hooky and Light Ale each won gold medals and earned the brewery the Achievement Award from the British Bottlers Institute.

New beer for a new generation

The birth of James Clarke's son George in 1997 was marked by the brewing of a special beer named Generation, suggesting that he might in time become the sixth generation of the family to run the Hook Norton Brewery. There will be no undue pressure on him, however, and when he is old enough to decide he will do so freely – except that like all his predecessors he will have grown up with the brewery and its family traditions as part of his everyday life.

Meanwhile the present generation faces the challenges of the future with quiet optimism and an unassuming confidence in their product. Their survival where many others have disappeared is the result of private ownership and the happy link between two brewing families. It probably also owes a lot to the fact that they have been content with a modest scale of operation, allowing them to go on using traditional methods while continually improving the quality and consistency of Hook Norton beer.

10
THE TIED ESTATE

Hook Norton pubs in 1999

Abthorpe	The New Inn
Adderbury	The Bell Inn
Aynho	The Great Western Arms
Balscote	The Butchers Arms
Banbury	The Coach and Horses
	Ye Olde Reindeer Inn
Blockley	The Great Western Arms
Bloxham	The Elephant and Castle
Brailes	The George Hotel
	The Gate Inn
Cherington	The Cherington Arms
Chipping Norton	The Albion Tavern
	The Fox Hotel
	The Red Lion
Chipping Warden	The Rose and Crown

A Country Brewery: Hook Norton 1849–1999

Deddington	The Crown and Tuns
Edgehill	The Castle Inn
Epwell	The Chandlers Arms
Evesham	The Trumpet
Great Bourton	The Bell Inn
Greatworth	The Inn
Grove	The Volunteer
Hook Norton	The Gate Hangs High
	The Pear Tree
	The Sun Inn
Ilmington	The Red Lion
Kings Sutton	The Butchers Arms
Leamington Spa	The Black Horse
Lower Boddington	The Carpenters Arms
Marston St Lawrence	The Marston Inn
Moreton in Marsh	The Wellington Inn
Newbold on Stour	The Bird in Hand
Shipston on Stour	The Coach and Horses
Stoke Lyne	The Peyton Arms
Sulgrave	The Star Inn
Thorpe Mandeville	The Three Conies
Wardington	The Hare and Hounds
Whatcote	The Royal Oak
Wigginton	The White Swan